GLOBAL REMIX

GLOBAL REMIX

The Fight for
Competitive Advantage

RICHARD SCASE

**KOGAN
PAGE**

London & Philadelphia

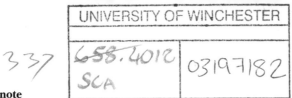

Publisher's note

Every possible effort has been made to ensure that the information contained in this book is accurate at the time of going to press, and the publishers and authors cannot accept responsibility for any errors or omissions, however caused. No responsibility for loss or damage occasioned to any person acting, or refraining from action, as a result of the material in this publication can be accepted by the editor, the publisher or the author.

First published in Great Britain and the United States in 2007 by Kogan Page Limited
Reprinted in 2007

120 Pentonville Road
London N1 9JN
United Kingdom
www.kogan-page.co.uk

525 South 4th Street, #241
Philadelphia PA 19147
USA

© Richard Scase, 2007

ISBN-10   0 7494 4871 7
ISBN-13   978 0 7494 4871 4

British Library Cataloguing-in-Publication Data

A CIP record for this book is available from the British Library.

Library of Congress Cataloging-in-Publication Data

Scase, Richard.
  Global remix : the fight for competitive advantage / Richard Scase.
    p. cm.
  Includes bibliographical references.
  ISBN 0–7494–4871–7
  1. Globalization–Economic aspects. 2. International business enterprises – Management. 3. Competition. 4. Strategic planning. I. Title.
HF1359.S2997 2007
337–dc22
                        2006026474

Typeset by Saxon Graphics Ltd, Derby
Printed and bound in Great Britain by MPG Books Ltd, Bodmin, Cornwall

Contents

Preface

Over the past 10 years or so I have been giving presentations across the world to corporate leaders and their management teams. In these I have endeavoured to analyse and discuss the major trends that are likely to impact on their organizations over the next 10 to 15 years. My aim is always to outline the broader global issues and then to narrow these down to more immediate business environments. In general terms, business speakers adopt one of two approaches. Either they focus upon major macro trends and devote little attention to the specific challenges facing their particular audiences, or, by emphasizing specific individual and organizational issues, they neglect broader market trends. In my talks I always try to do both, combining both approaches. This is the inspiration behind the preparation of this book.

Its distinctive feature is that it discusses the direction of broader global business trends and how these, over the next one to two decades, are likely to impact upon both our businesses and ourselves, as individuals.

Global business is being restructured through the rise of India and China and the other Asian economies. This is leading to the shift of mass manufacturing to these countries. It is also having a major impact on energy and commodity prices. The world runs out of oil in 40 years' time. China now accounts for one-third of the annual increase in global oil consumption. The US trade deficit is partly caused by the export of goods from US-owned companies in China to consumers in the United States.

Alongside this, there is in the West the break-up of the old marketing categories based on age, occupation and income. The liberated consumer forms diverse and ever-changing niches that can only be reached through long-tail marketing strategies. Consumer technologies are reinforcing this trend. This changing business environment demands that companies reinvent themselves if they are to succeed.

At the corporate level, the book outlines the factors required for competitive advantage. These are based on developing creative cultures that lead to the rollout of innovative products and services. This demands the rejection of business models that are based on line management techniques. Young talent – the iPod generation – will not be told what to do and yet their creative ideas are the drivers of future competitive advantage. This will demand a new business model that encourages sociability and informality, what I call the 'café corporation'.

The problem is that management training on executive programmes and in business schools does not encourage the development of personal talents that allow corporations to operate in this way. Both private and public sector organizations need more leaders and fewer managers. To operate as café corporations, they need to reinvent their structures with very small operating units and drastically new cultures. The corporate elephants need to take some lessons from smaller entrepreneurial fleas, the flourishing small business sectors that are driving economic growth in many countries. In the future, large corporations will be disaggregated as collections of small business units operating under well-known brands. Few companies in Europe and the United States today meet these criteria.

Twenty-first-century employees will need to reinvent themselves continually if they are to survive in this new corporate world. Qualifications obtained in devalued education and university systems are no longer enough. We have to identify and develop our own unique personal skills. The café corporation will employ just three kinds of people: celebrities, lieutenants and 'passing through' strangers. Which of these we are will shape our earnings, lifestyles and personal relationships. More of us will have to be celebrities and 'passing through' strangers and fewer of us will be needed as lieutenants – the declining bastions of old management structures and cultures.

In the preparation of this book the intention has been to combine a rigorous analytical approach with a written style that is both easy to read and entertaining. In striving to achieve this, I have drawn upon my experiences as an entrepreneur, academic researcher and corporate speaker. This book is dedicated to all those business leaders and managers whose day-to-day experiences act out, in very real ways, the major socio-economic trends that are shaping the direction of business life in the first decades of the 21st century.

Acknowledgements

This book has evolved out of the many corporate presentations I have been giving over the past ten years. These have been in all places of the world and range from small workshops with corporate leaders through to mega industry and professional events with sometimes more than a thousand delegates. It is to these I am indebted through the challenging questions they put to me either under the glare of the spotlight in front of their professional colleagues or more informally during coffee breaks. I also owe a great debt to Paul Tyrrell who worked with me on the preparation of this book and to Jonathan Scales. But I owe most to Brendan Barns and his colleagues Tracey Ball and Steve Chamberlain at Speakers for Business for their constant encouragement and support. Thanks are due to all these varied inputs. However, I take full responsibility for the ideas discussed, some of which may seem crazy but if they contribute to debate and discussion about the future of business, this book will have achieved its purpose.

For more information on Professor Richard Scase's work please visit www.richardscase.com

Richard is exclusively represented by:

SPEAKERS for BUSINESS
1–2 Pudding Lane
London EC3R 8AB
United Kingdom
Tel: +44 (0)20 7929 5559
Fax: +44 (0)20 7929 5558
E-mail: richard@richardscase.com
Website: www.sfb.com

1 Global appetites, local tastes

West is East and East is West

- Global convergence – the internet and worldwide supply chains
- China – the world's dominant economy
- India – straight into the knowledge economy
- 2.5 billion consumers into the global economy – business opportunities for Western companies
- Not quite the death of distance – trust, face-to-face and competitive clusters
- Should we all learn Mandarin?

The rise of the economies of India and China is sending shock waves throughout the boardrooms of Western companies. Sure, it's proving a threat to the leaders of many industries, not least because it represents a vast reservoir of (comparatively) cheap labour. But above all it's an opportunity – according to Goldman Sachs, by 2020 consumers in India and China will have the highest aggregate purchasing power of any regional population in the world. Maybe your company will generate most of its future growth from the West, but chances are you will need to look in the opposite direction as well.

The most successful companies over the next few decades will be those that search farthest and widest for growth opportunities, extra efficiencies and valuable groups of consumers they can aggregate using the latest information and communication technologies. You just need to acknowledge that the number of market niches immune to global trends is tiny, and diminishing fast. Most companies, especially those in the West, are now 'international' by default. So if you aren't trading or collaborating with business partners overseas you need to, start pretty soon. Otherwise two things will happen: 1) your capacity for international growth will be jeopardized and 2) you'll end up losing ground to cannier rivals in your domestic markets.

May Day protestors give the impression that globalization could be 'switched off' or reversed if only the world's most powerful countries would pull the right levers. However, in reality, the trend is self-fuelling, destined to move faster and become more entrenched. Why? Because communication is an insatiable desire for everyone on the planet, whether you are settling differences or exchanging goods, and every type of communication is advancing at unprecedented speed. Telecommunications such as mobile phones and the internet, physical communications such as airports and container hubs – all are enabling business practices to be standardized and harmonized internationally. More fundamentally, they're enabling the majority of companies in the West and a burgeoning number in the East to buy from and sell to anywhere on the planet, with ever-increasing speed and efficiency.

The internet is, of course, the public face of this new-found interconnectedness. It's also the most empowering communications tool devised. Any company with a computer, a web browser, a modem and access to a phone line can now: look worldwide for the components and talent it needs to build innovative products and services; market itself worldwide in a cost-effective manner; and fulfil orders quickly and reliably using outsourced credit verification, escrow and delivery services.

Medium and large-sized companies can situate different units of their operation in different places – to benefit from lower

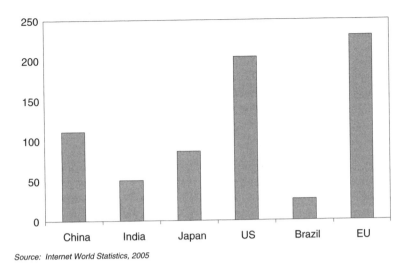

Source: *Internet World Statistics, 2005*

Figure 1.1   Internet penetration 2005 (million)

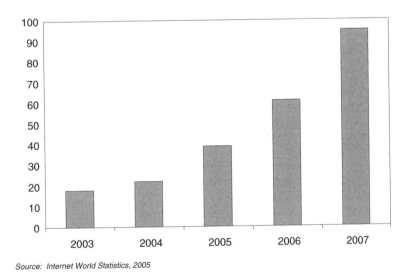

Source: *Internet World Statistics, 2005*

Figure 1.2   India internet users (million)

wages, local government incentives or unique expertise – while at the same time managing these units as if they were situated on a single site.[1]

The bigger a company grows, the more it can seek out extra efficiencies through disaggregation or collaboration abroad. It must do these things, because bigness doesn't guarantee strength any more – as we'll discuss in Chapter 2, 'economies of scale' and 'barriers to entry' don't scare entrepreneurs when even the smallest company can afford to harness global supply chains and seek out customers for its highly personalized services or highly customized products. Cross-border mergers and acquisitions will continue as established corporations from the West seek to restructure themselves and rising corporations in the East stake their claim to markets to which they previously had no access. It's this international flow of capital that gave rise to global supply chains in the first place and created a sustainable business case for the internet to boot. In the coming decades it will involve so much business that economic cycles will no longer be confined to national boundaries.

Consider the present-day G8. A few of the world's richest nations are present, but not all of them. In the coming decades, if the membership list stays as it is today, it will be even more unrepresentative. The investment bank Goldman Sachs predicts that by 2050 the qualifying countries (in terms of GDP (gross domestic product) at purchasing power parity) should be China, the United States, India, Japan, Brazil, Russia, the UK and Germany, in that order.

Some strategists and statisticians believe that India will be on a more equal footing with China, or even surpass it, because it has a higher number of English speakers, and because its demographics suggest that its working population could outnumber that of China by 2030. Nevertheless, everyone agrees that, by 2020 at the latest, China and India should each have a seat at the G8 table.

If you believe that today's G8 sets the agenda for world business, with an impact on even the smallest companies, can you put yourself ahead of the game by looking at the countries that will be its most influential members in two decades' time or later?

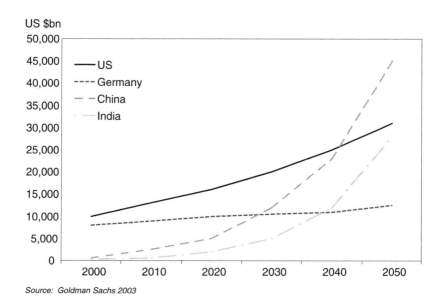

Figure 1.3   The future is Asia (projected GDP)

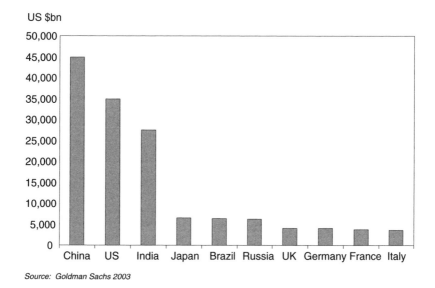

Figure 1.4   The largest economies in 2050 (GDP 2003 US $bn)

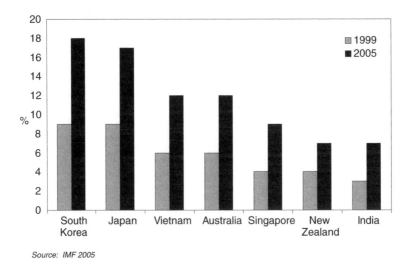

Source: IMF 2005

Figure 1.5 The knock-on effect of China's growth: trade with China as a % of total merchandise trade

Unquestionably, yes. You just need to understand how the economies of India and China have reached the point they are at today, and what 'sure things' are visible in their future. Then you can take steps to share in their success.

If you want to see the future look East

Offshoring has been the scourge of Western manufacturing bosses, union leaders and some politicians in recent years. It's the most vivid demonstration of modern trade integration and corporate mobility – a necessary but painful step towards a more level playing field for individuals as well as businesses across the world. Yet it's actually nothing new. Large companies in the West began offshoring facilities to Taiwan in the 1960s; US electronics company Texas Instruments did the same in Bangalore, India, back in 1984. What's caught everyone by surprise since the 1990s is the speed at which offshoring has taken hold. Again, it's the advance of networking technologies that is to blame (or to praise, if your company is sufficiently forward-looking). Equally crucial has been the progress made by China in moving its economy towards a market socialist system. Today both India and China are seeking to consolidate their image as the offshoring destinations of choice for Western companies by investing heavily in education and infrastructure.

Don't expect wages to rise significantly in either country any time soon. Their combined population is so great, at around 2.5 billion people, that it'll take decades for scarcity value to be a factor in this equation.

By 2020, Asia will be the predominant choice for any Western company wishing to offshore production. For any large company it will, in fact, be best practice to send to the East all but the most specialized, brand-influencing and location-critical activities. Clearly, this will create problems for unskilled workers – the world will be so integrated that companies will find it easier to buy in skills from the cheapest possible source. It will therefore be the responsibility of governments and the number-one career goal of individuals in the richest economies to develop skills, knowledge resources and experience that are difficult to duplicate.

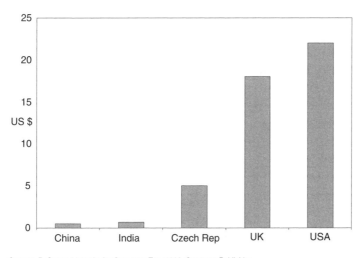

Source: R. Scase, *Living in the Corporate Zoo*, 2002, Capstone Publishing

Figure 1.6   Hourly labour costs in manufacturing sector 2005

China's special economic zones (SEZs) along its eastern coast have attracted huge inward foreign direct investment, while the country as a whole has become the manufacturing base of the world. Already China produces roughly 90 per cent of the world's PCs. Samsung Electronics has ceased its production of notebook computers in South Korea and relocated to China. According to the *Financial Times* (March 2006), Beijing plans to build a US $300 million computer chip manufacturing plant, emphasizing its commitment to become a global semiconductor manufacturing centre. Over the next few years many of China's new private enterprises will transform from contractors into global market-leading brands.

Some of these brands have the resources to acquire businesses in the West and couple them with production efficiencies at home. The Chinese computer manufacturer Lenovo, for example, acquired IBM's personal computing division in December 2004 for US $1.75 billion in what is seen as an epoch-making deal. Other brands are acquiring foreign rivals for their research and development expertise, creative abilities or knowledge of local markets. The home appliance manufacturer Haier, for example, acquired the refrigerator division of the Italian company Meneghetti in 2001, because it has a reputation for products that are stylish and technologically groundbreaking.

Meanwhile, India has a number of attractions for Western companies beyond its low labour costs. It has a prodigious work ethic. It also has a huge English-speaking population – indeed, its impressive higher education system creates around a million English-speaking graduates every year. By 2008, it will have more technology graduates than the populations of many European countries, including the UK, France, Italy and Spain. All these things, in concert with wages that are still comparatively low, mean that India is already in a great position to take service jobs away from the West. Indeed, McKinsey and Co has estimated that 10 per cent of accountancy and legal jobs in the United States will be outsourced to India by 2010.

The reaction to this inexorable trend has, again, been hysterical in many Western countries, particularly the United States, where both Republicans and Democrats have advocated protectionist policies specifically to counter what they perceive to be the 'Indian threat'. Paul Craig Roberts, a former economic adviser to Ronald Reagan, gave a speech in January 2004 to the Brookings Institution in Washington, DC in which he suggested that, because of offshoring: 'The United States will be a Third-World country in 20 years.' Yet there is much evidence to suggest that the phenomenon is, in general, healthy for the US economy. A 2002 survey by US management consultants McKinsey & Co found that wages for data entry personnel in India were US $2, a tenth of the equivalent wage paid in the United States. At the same time it calculated that for every dollar a US company offshores it gets a net cost reduction of 58 cents, while the US economy gets a US $1.14 dollar benefit (not least because its consumers can buy goods at lower prices).

What the United States should really be worried about is the rising number of Indian companies that are challenging Western brands in the service industries. The country's software industry is poised for major growth – it will have exports of US $90 billion by 2008 – and companies such as Infosys Technologies in Bangalore, Satyam Computer Services in Hyderabad and Tata Consultancy Services in Mumbai are not scared of the dominant Western players in their industry. They certainly don't regard themselves as the custodians of low-margin business, entrusting all matters of creativity, design and innovation to their First World 'superiors'.

One-half of India's 1.2-billion-strong population is under 25 years old, and its education system is improving in leaps and bounds. Its high-school students may have a lower average level of ability than their US counterparts right now, according to the latest Trends in International Mathematics and Science Study (TIMSS), carried out in 2003, but in the coming decades it will undoubtedly have a higher number of talented youngsters in absolute terms. (It's also worth pointing out that although the United States showed an improvement in this TIMSS survey over previous years, its fourth-graders (aged 9–10) were still outperformed by those of Taiwan, Japan and Singapore.)

Both India and China are developing highly educated, highly qualified scientists and technologists in huge numbers. They are becoming leaders in research areas from pharmaceuticals to biotechnology. As a result, the jobs in the West that used to offer the highest rewards will soon be among the most vulnerable to offshoring. We are witnessing the start of a shift in the knowledge economy's balance of power, one that will eventually lead to a brain drain from West to East, as Asia becomes the world's main source of entrepreneurial growth opportunities.[2]

Alongside this growing appetite for talent is a growing appetite for raw materials and energy. China in particular already accounts for a high proportion of the world's steel and iron ore consumption. In 2005 this was almost one-half of the world's consumption of coal and iron ore and 20 per cent of steel, aluminium, copper and zinc. This clearly has a major impact on worldwide commodity prices. More significantly, its oil consumption is greatly outstripping oil production, a factor behind the desperate bid for US producer Unocal in June 2005 by the China National Offshore Oil Corporation (CNOOC). Since 2001, Chinese oil consumption has increased by more than 40 per cent, accounting for one-third of the total growth in worldwide oil demand.

Today, China consumes 7 million barrels per day, making it the world's second-largest consumer and third-largest importer

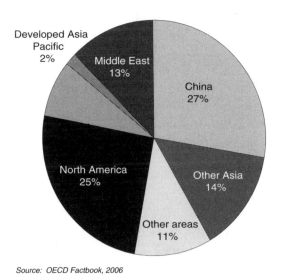

Source: OECD Factbook, 2006

Figure 1.7 Share of oil growth in consumption (from 2002 to 2005 – %)

after the United States and Japan. In the coming decades, the issue of where China gets its oil will have a heavy influence on world politics and prices, whether it searches in the Middle East, in territory whose ownership is disputed by Japan or in Africa and other places. It has signed a long-term supply deal worth US $70 billion with Iran. The US Energy Information Administration has estimated that China's demand for oil will more than double by 2025, reaching 14 million barrels a day, of which roughly two-thirds will be imported.

Notwithstanding this tension, we know that the world's oil supply is quickly running out. Every company should therefore be thinking now about how its local fuel and energy prices are likely to change in the long term. Obviously, petrol will remain of primary importance for several decades – in Europe and the United States the price per litre/gallon will treble by 2015 – although some energy commentators expect demand for crude oil to peak at around 110 million barrels per day in 2020, as reserves dwindle and supra-national agreements on carbon

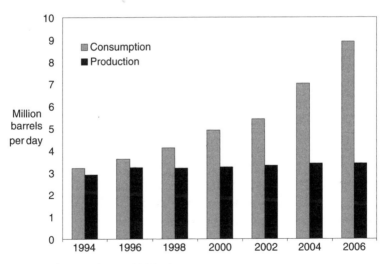

Source: US Energy Information Administration

Figure 1.8   China's oil production and consumption 1994–2006

reduction begin to bite. Whether gas or some other source of energy becomes the global benchmark at this point, it is generally agreed that overall energy prices will continue to rise steadily. The demands of Asia will continue to outstrip supply, as they are already doing in other areas of business – China's importing of raw materials and exporting of finished products, for example, is to blame for much of the increase in shipping costs that has occurred in recent years.

So, the (relatively short) march of the Asian economies is about to enter its decisive phase: we've already witnessed the wholesale transfer of manufacturing operations to India and China, and of data services to India. Right now we're seeing consumer services flow into India and China by virtue of their growing middle-class populations; from around 2015 onwards, we'll see the core of the knowledge economy shifting eastwards. Those of us already doing business in the UK, Europe and the United States can only acknowledge that the shift is under way and prepare accordingly. But we should do so with excitement rather than fear: China and India may be getting more competitive but they're also getting richer, and that means selling opportunities. The playing field of global business is becoming wider and more level (albeit with big divots and on uneven ground), and this should mean more prosperity for everyone.

Say 'namasté' and 'ni hao' to two billion potential customers

Can India and China really still be classed as 'developing' countries? Only in the sense that they each still have huge numbers living in poverty and at the mercy of agriculture. Even so, the World Bank estimates that China's rural poverty population dropped from 280 million in 1990 to 124 million in 1997, a decrease of 55.7 per cent, and various surveys since suggest that its overall poverty level is now falling even faster. India is still much poorer, with about 25 per cent of its 1.2-billion-strong population still below the poverty line, but the compound annual growth rate of its GDP in the period 1994–2004 was around 6.8 per cent, while the level of poverty dropped over the same period by around 10 percentage points. It has created a group of consumers able and eager to buy Western brands for the first time. This urban middle class appears to be adopting all the same spending patterns as its Western equivalent. It also includes a highly mobile elite that regularly visits the capitals of Western countries for conspicuous consumption. Like their European counterparts, Indian and Chinese yuppies are seizing the earliest opportunity to buy into the American ideals of copious entertainment, abundant food choices and domestic convenience.

So we arrive at another compelling reason why Western companies – particularly those medium or large in size – should be offshoring business units to Asia, or setting up new ones there. By doing so, they can build a strong presence and localized expertise in markets where they expect the strongest growth. This was a key factor behind the offshoring plans of the British banking giant HSBC when, in March 2004, it announced it would offshore 4,000 jobs from the UK. The country that has done most to integrate itself into the Asian business community is, of course, the United States. It has created 350,000 registered companies, partnerships and joint ventures in China, while the rest of the world has created only 150,000. Indeed, some Western countries are lagging far behind – only 1 per cent of the UK's total exports currently goes to India and China, which in view of its historical relations with these countries is a poor figure. Asia is courting foreign investment at such speed that no company can afford to spend the traditional three to five years planning to export there, nor to wait for encouragement, support or incentives from their governments.

The rewards for those that move quickly and sensibly enough are likely to be high. A 2004 report from Goldman Sachs predicted that, in the so-called BRICs economies (those of Brazil, Russia, India and China), the number of people with an income of more than US $3,000 – 'a level consistent with entry into the "middle class"' – could be 800 million by 2014. 'In China alone, the number of people with incomes over US $3,000 could increase by close to 10 times in the next decade and by nearly 14 times in India, though off a much lower base,' it said. 'In Brazil, that number could more than double.' The report added that, 'by 2025, there could be more than 200 million new people (more than the population of Japan) in these economies with incomes above US $15,000, up from a tiny fraction today'. Clearly, this represents a huge opportunity for industries such as professional services, entertainment, the media, healthcare and retail – industries in which Western companies have traditionally been dominant. Sure, the BRICs economies will produce an increasing number of home-grown companies in these sectors, but for the time being the West has experience on its side, as well as deeper pockets for corporate venturing.

In other industries, Indian and Asian consumption patterns look set to conform to historical norms. The car is still the clear-est symbol of emergent mass affluence, and by 2025 the Chinese will be buying around 200 million of them a year – more than any other country. The urban areas of India and China are moving faster up the 'hierarchy of needs' at unprecedented speed, and as a result their cosmopolitan young professionals are already acquiring the disposable income to make sizeable lifestyle purchases in sectors such as fashion, household furnish-ings, leisure and beauty products.

The West is likely to find big opportunities and high margins in these sectors, as young people in Asia are still predominantly led by Western tastes, and particularly by those of the United States and Europe. When we say globalization, for the most part we really mean Americanization, in terms of not only corporate brands but also the music, films and television shows it has exported so successfully. It is the media that have created the global village, and the world's most influential media companies are still clustered around New York City and Los Angeles. A cat-alyst for this adoption of Western lifestyles will be the increase in tourism from East to West resulting from rising incomes and the increased competitiveness of air travel. By 2015, around 100 million Chinese tourists will travel to foreign countries every year.

Similarly, an increased number of Asian students will come to the West for higher education. Already they are taking MBAs at

Australian, UK and US universities in large numbers, absorbing the latest business knowledge and then taking it home, to apply entrepreneurially in growth markets more dynamic than any still nascent in the West. Education, therefore, is another sector in which the West should maintain its thought leadership and, for a while at least, its commercial dominance.

Why you need a personal touch in global markets

Millions of manufacturing jobs have already moved East, millions of service jobs are about to do the same, and all the while management theorists are droning on about how this represents 'best practice' for Western companies and economies. But what about the cost to Western individuals? Is every job in the United States and Europe now at risk, if India and China are breeding experts in even the most technical and expert fields?

Certainly, Western companies will be exposed to more competition in the future – that's what having a level playing field is all about. But even the 'victims' of globalization in the West have benefited from the phenomenon in several ways. Chief among these is lower prices: the wholesale shift of manufacturing to Asia has helped to control inflation, and to reduce the prices of a variety of household items, including white goods, clothing and telecommunications equipment. Take a look at the country of origin of TV sets, hi-fi equipment, DVD players, garden furniture and yes, even '19th century furniture' exported from Europe to the United States: 'Made in China'.[3] As a result, almost everyone in the world – barring those in failed states – has found it easier to improve their quality of life.

Equally, Western workers shouldn't be afraid of losing their job through the disintermediation made possible by information and communication technologies. Just as the paperless office has remained largely a myth, so too has the idea of business without personal contact. Trading internationally means building up relationships with contractors and subcontractors, and for most businesspeople a face-to-face meeting is still one of the prerequisites of trust. It also means educating managers about foreign business practices, regulations and trends – preferably by flying them to key emerging markets on a regular basis. At the same time, it is necessary to recruit new senior executives from key growth markets, to help plug gaps in organizational knowledge. In any event, human contact will remain the best way to ensure both strategic alignment and compliance across globally distributed business units, particularly when conflicting national regulations threaten the integrity of, say, customer data and intellectual property rights. The overwhelming majority of businesses, both large and small, are having to be 'internationalized' in their cultures and working practices.

Regional customs will also put the onus on relationships. In China, for example, the business world is underpinned by the principle of 'guanxi' (which literally means 'relationships'). It holds that any business deal should be preceded by personal contact between individuals, so those involved can gauge one another's compatibility and trustworthiness. Since global supply chains tend to rely on large numbers of contracting and subcontracting arrangements – in which the identity of ultimate parent companies is not necessarily clear – the management of relationships is already a crucial discipline for companies operating in Asia. Western companies need to make sure they understand how to foster trust, because they have grown out of a business culture whose boundaries are defined largely by contracts and commercial law rather than personal networks.[4]

As the need for cross-border bonding grows, so it will generate business of its own, not only in terms of travel services, hotels and hospitality but also in the support services built around travel hubs such as cleaning and maintenance agencies, supermarkets and petrol stations. Even unskilled workers should be able to find regular work here, albeit of the transitory, 'McJob' variety. At the same time, some of the most secure jobs in the West will be in trades such as plumbing, electrical work and decorating – an irony considering that most Western education systems have been geared firmly towards the knowledge industries for many years. As we'll discuss in Chapter 3, it is the tradespeople who can afford to feel most secure because their skills are intrinsically linked to physical locations. Will it be better to be a hairdresser or plumber than an accountant or design engineer?

Trades and crafts are, in any case, poised to undergo a mini-Renaissance in the West as people spend more money on expressing themselves through home interiors, clothes and other material possessions. Just as Asian young professionals are buying into Western tastes, so Western young professionals are seeking to differentiate themselves even further from their peers through what they regard as tasteful, self-defining purchases. It's just one symptom of a phenomenon dubbed 'New Luxury', under which people in affluent societies free up cash for non-essentials as goods previously deemed luxurious become cheaper. For example, cheaper flights have led us to spend more on hotels, while cheaper white goods have led us to spend more on home décor. They/we can thank China for that.

The home-improvement boom is endless in the United States and Europe, fuelled in part by booming property prices. Barring any disastrous economic downturn that lowers discretionary spending across the world, the lifestyle industries should be able to recycle their product and service offerings continuously, in line with prevailing fashions. It's a subject we'll return to in Chapter 6. For the time being, companies can grow either by identifying a product or service that is linked intrinsically to a particular location, or by aggregating groups of consumers across the world who have very specific needs or tastes. These will be the chief growth models for any company in the future.

The dangers of ubiquity are, of course, well known to the world's biggest brands. It's a rule of thumb for luxury goods manufacturers that a total brand value of US $2 billion represents a tipping point beyond which they can no longer call themselves 'exclusive'. Equally, brands that are conspicuously American have become more vulnerable in recent years to globalized boycotting (see Chapter 7). Thankfully for all these brands, the technologies allowing small companies to act big are also allowing big companies to act small. They have enabled the creation of highly efficient inventory management among retailers, lean production systems and flexible assembly processes that make it cost-effective to produce highly localized or even personalized goods. Someone who wishes to buy a car, for example, can now do so in many cases by submitting a detailed specification to a retailer, who then alerts the manufacturer to schedule production on the basis of component orders placed with globally distributed suppliers. However, it will always be easier for smaller companies to offer more exclusivity, either through highly customized products or highly personalized services. Even small manufacturers in the West may be able to compete with the economies of scale achieved by their Asian counterparts if they can find a creative enough way to exploit their assets.

It's a myth of the knowledge economy that any organization can operate from anywhere provided it has sufficiently reliable communications links. Companies are finding that their core workers, upon whom they rely for their most innovative products and services, are attaching an increasing level of importance to where they live. This is another natural consequence of mass affluence – as individuals grow more experienced and more aware of their value to employers, so they expect to be rewarded with a higher quality of life, and this depends on the amenities and 'buzz' of their locality as much as the proximity of friends and family. As we'll discuss in Chapter 2, senior executives will have to be mindful of the lifestyles of core workers, as well as the potential for offshore efficiencies, in the way they structure their companies.

Clustering: how to get by with a little help from your rivals

Another way in which local areas will be crucial to global business is through the growth and creation of what Harvard professor Michael Porter has dubbed 'clusters'; groups of companies from the same or similar industries that find it mutually beneficial to gather in specific places. In the past, clusters were based on the local availability of raw materials, energy sources and transport facilities – that's why places such as Pittsburgh, Chicago, Glasgow, Alsace Lorraine, Lancashire and the Ruhr Valley developed the way they did during the Industrial Revolution. Today, global forces have just as much influence over the formation of clusters as local ones.

Look at the business world from a distance and you'll see that companies in many industries still cluster around natural resources – oil and gas companies in the Middle East; coffee-growers in South America; diamond-miners in Russia, India and South Africa. Zoom in and you'll see the odd country specializing in particular industries, as the result of a historical legacy or a conscious effort on the part of the government to consolidate the achievements of its most successful companies.[5] Zoom in further and you'll begin to see true clusters in the sense that Michael Porter describes them. The members of these vertical networks have moved closer together, or established themselves alongside rivals they wish to unseat, to make a variety of things easier: the transfer of business, money and materials; joint or collaborative ventures; and the attraction of customers, who obviously like to be able to shop around without travelling too far.

Some local clusters are old and robust, such as the financial districts of the world, which after several hundred years retain their clout. More recent examples include Silicon Valley in California. Others are less well known but growing in influence: for example, information and communication technology companies have flocked to Boston, Massachusetts; the Antwerp–Brussels corridor in Belgium; Helsinki in Finland; Stockholm in Sweden; and the Cambridge Fens in the UK. Certain ancillary industries have also formed their own clusters – for example, the need to 'localize' US products and services for different national business requirements has generated a cluster of software design skills around Dublin in the Republic of Ireland.

In some cases, clusters self-organize thanks to an influx of similar companies or orders. Thus, Accra in Ghana has become known for its data-processing activities, thanks to offshoring by European and US companies; while the town of Novosibirsk in Siberia, Russia, is emerging as a centre for software design because of outsourcing by German corporations. Elsewhere, governments are taking active steps to promote the birth of clusters. China, for example, has lavished investment on the Tianjin Hi-Tech Industry Development Zone, a short distance south-east of Beijing, which has infrastructure and facilities to rival anything in the West. Similarly, India has promoted the growth of its call centre cluster in Bangalore.

No matter what their origins, clusters will need a growing amount of support and promotion in the coming decades, if they are to retain their pre-eminence and a corresponding long-term revenue stream. Global mobility that encourages companies to create jobs in certain countries also allows them to take jobs away at a moment's notice, with profit-making centres set up and demolished according to short-term profit calculations. Today's global corporate capitalists seem to have little of the affinity or social responsibility their entrepreneurial predecessors showed towards local communities. This is not surprising given the growing distance between senior corporate decision-makers and their operational staff, and the tendency of institutional shareholders to act with dispassionate Darwinism.

Nevertheless, clusters represent one of the best ways to prevent massive lay-offs, and to ameliorate the effects of redundancies should they occur. As talent pools, they can consolidate their expertise in particular industries. As employment pools, they are the best place for sacked specialists to find new jobs. Of course, they can have the stuffing knocked out of them if a sufficiently large adverse trend comes along – Silicon Valley, for example, suffered disproportionately after the dotcom bubble burst in 2001. Yet even there, the technologists and venture capitalists have returned, in recognition of the fact that an address in the area is effectively a hallmark for innovative high-tech thinking. The cluster was strong enough to break and heal with greater strength, and the prospective investors pouring into the Valley today know that any entrepreneurs still there are likely to be much wiser than they were in the 1990s. Perhaps the biggest contribution to the dotcom crash was blithe optimism on the part of company bosses, who were disconnected completely from the reality of their non-paying customer bases. Better than anyone, they know that, to succeed in today's knowledge economy, a company must build a relationship with a group of customers that is as tightly defined as possible, and listen carefully to ensure that these customers feel well served.

Endnotes

1 Growth through internationalization: Babel Media is a British software engineering company providing localization and porting services to computer games developers. Its young, multilingual staff translate in-game dialogue and ensures that new titles operate on a variety of gaming platforms – a new type of service ancillary to a burgeoning industry. The company employs around 300 people in four locations: 1) Hove, a town on the south coast of England near Brighton, chosen because among UK conurbations it has the second-largest concentration of foreign students after London; 2) New Delhi, chosen for its English-speaking graduate population willing to work for low wages; 3) Los Angeles, chosen for its proximity to some of the world's major games developers, and to provide a more attentive service to principal clients; and 4) Montreal, chosen because of a generous subsidy from the Quebec government, under which firms that help to produce interactive software can claim back up to 30 per cent of the salaries of their production staff – an incentive that has created one of the world's pre-eminent clusters of computer games technology.

2 The liberation of Asia's entrepreneurs: It is not only Western entrepreneurs who are capitalizing on the reduced cost of entry to most markets created by the revolution in information and communication technologies. Asia too has plenty of young professionals with language skills keen to set up their own businesses, and they are growing in number all the time. Take, for example, a software design business in Fiji which has 20 employees serving financial institutions in the United States, the UK and Australia – it proves that even specialists in Western service companies face the kind of 'creative destruction' predicted by the economist Joseph Schumpeter in 1934, because their small rivals now have access to the same networks while benefiting from lower overheads in their local areas.

3   A small business in the south of England trades from a shed selling '19th-century British furniture'. Eighty per cent of its products are made in China and 70 per cent exported to the United States, selling online to mid-West customers.

4   Bridging the trust gap: Alibaba is the world's largest trade 'bulletin board system', a means for businesses in any country to specify goods they wish to buy or sell. Headquartered in Hangzhou, China, it has around 2,400 staff and 18 million registered users. Much of the site's revenue comes from a facility called 'TrustPass', under which sellers pay an annual fee of US $349 to authenticate their identity and provide detailed information about their businesses, thereby helping to foster trust and quicken the set-up of trading relationships.

5   For example, Singapore – value-added logistics; Italy – design; India – software; Asia – manufacture; United States – information services; Africa – commodities and agriculture; South America – commodities and manufacture; Europe – high technology; Middle East – oil and intellectual capital.

2 Is your company doomed – at least in its present form?

<hr>

Times they are a-changing – it really is the 21st century

- It's the corporate brand that does it
- Globalized resources for localized performance
- How am I going to work in these new business structures?
- Corporate celebrities, lieutenants, stalwarts, travellers and orphans – which one am I?
- So we have to be nice to each other if the business is to innovate
- The war for talent – and they won't be told what to do

<hr>

How many limbs could you hack off your company before it ceased to be distinguishable from any other? Make a list right now. Chances are, they are the business units you'll need to outsource (or, at least, streamline through collaboration with other organizations) by 2020. Why? Because your rivals are doing the same to become more efficient than you. Then they'll pump the money they save back into their core competencies. Then they'll dismember your company on your behalf, starting with the customer-base.

'Who are these rivals?' you may ask. 'Surely if I identify them now, I can tailor my defences accordingly, or get rid of them with a pre-emptive strike.' Well, maybe. A few will certainly be familiar because you've shared your cosy, domestic markets with them for many years. But there is another, more deadly, species lurking just around the corner – the young entrepreneur operating from a cost-optimal location (probably not in the West), with all your company's talent but none of its baggage.

The communications revolution has lowered the barriers to entry in most industries and given every business near-limitless geographical reach. Your company faces ever-increasing competition from all over the world. In this context, if you think a reactive strategy will protect your market share, you should expect to end up as capitalist road-kill: rival companies won't need to hunt you down, they'll simply flatten you with their progress.

Of course, a global marketplace is only useful if its prospective buyers can find the prospective sellers they need. This is why internet search engines such as Google have achieved dizzying valuations. It follows that companies with higher marketing budgets should be able to draw more custom. However, the world's most affluent consumers today (but maybe not tomorrow) – young professionals in the West – are becoming more fickle. Size impresses them less now than it used to, partly as a result of brand ubiquity and ethical boycotting, but mainly because, in a global village where cultures homogenize quickly, they are continually seeking to differentiate themselves from their peers.

The power of word-of-mouth marketing is growing as advances continue to be made in networking technology, and as consumers find new ways to exchange information online. Furthermore, quality is no longer the differentiator it once was. In most industries – particularly those that are service-based – consumers have an array of reputable suppliers from whom to buy. The communications revolution has brought some industries to a plateau of efficiency and quality, beyond which their constituent companies must innovate continuously to attract and retain customers.

Doing things better than everyone else no longer guarantees a market-leading position – it merely gets you to the starting grid. To be competitive, you need to do things differently, by applying the creativity of your best innovators to the upcoming needs and desires of core markets. When Apple adopted the phrase 'Think Different' in 1997 as its marketing slogan for the Macintosh computer, it was among the first major corporations to face these issues on a global scale. At the time, the pre-eminence of its operating system, which had always been highly regarded thanks to its versatility and ease of use, was being challenged by the best-selling Microsoft application *Windows 95*. Apple counter-attacked with a TV and cinema campaign that featured black-and-white footage of visionaries such as Einstein, Martin Luther King and Richard Branson, accompanied by a laudatory voiceover and followed by the slogan under the Apple logo, which at the time was bursting with colour.

The goals of the campaign were clear: 1) to co-opt the values of iconoclastic figures, making it clear that Apple was the choice of rebellious, creative and, by default, 'cool' people; 2) to associate the rarity of such people with the rarity of Apple's products in terms of market share, boosting their scarcity value; and, most significantly, 3) to create an emotional bond with the viewer, to persuade them that Apple shared any visionary, left-field, ambitious and life-affirming ambitions they might have. Can you honestly say your company understands and champions the desires of its customers in this way?

If not, you need to try harder. And don't make the excuse that you're not in the business of manufacturing sexy consumer gadgets. The Virgin Group was originally a record retailer, now it encompasses airline services, financial products and mobile phones. Most of what it offers is intangible, yet its brand is associated with fun and quality, largely as a result of Richard Branson's eccentric, passionate leadership. Virgin was one of the first and most successful adopters of a strategy that has now become commonplace: anchoring a brand in its values rather than in the products and services it sells.

Companies that ensure their brand is associated primarily with experiences – such as authenticity, trust or simply the promise of a higher quality of life – keep their options open. They can continually reinvent their portfolios of products or services, especially now that internet and communications technologies (ICTs) enable them to replace links of their supply chain more rapidly than ever before. They can tailor products and services to small groups or even individuals. Indeed, they must customize their offerings as far as possible, based on the detailed tracking and forecasting of customer preferences, if they wish to maximize their profits. In the new global marketplace, individuality is one of the most valuable commodities, and, thanks to ICT advances, one of the best ways to create new markets is via the aggregation of niche consumers in different countries.

Preparing for 2020 therefore requires two continuous, parallel efforts: 1) clarifying what you stand for; and 2) clarifying whom you're selling to, even if you're expanding your overall customer-base through the creation of sub-brands. It is only by ensuring you are the best-placed business to serve the needs of specific markets, and by communicating that fact effectively, that you can guarantee your survival.

These efforts make your company what it is, so they can't be outsourced completely. Nor should they be, unless they require major realignment to generate a new market (for example, in the case of a manufacturing firm that has substantial fixed assets but is reliant on a product fast becoming obsolete). Richard Branson exemplifies what Virgin stands for by being an adventurous, good-humoured and uncompromising bon viveur – when he finally quits, the brand will suffer if a similar successor cannot be found. It is his vision, and that of the senior managers he recruited, that defines Virgin's vision.

Equally, a company clarifies its identity in the way it interprets customer data. Many stages in the collection and analysis of such data can be outsourced, but ultimately a company's leaders must use it to innovate. It is by nailing this process that companies such as 3M, BP and Universal have become agile in the constant renewal of their product portfolios. Or take Centrica; it used to be a British state-owned utility company (British Gas), now it has mined its customer knowledge to become a highly diversified service provider, with offerings ranging from home insurance to credit cards and domestic repairs.

So we come to another of the paradoxes of globalized business: the wider the geographical spread of your company, the greater potential you have to consolidate its core. At the same time, a well-managed supply chain will help you to gather localized customer data and aggregate groups of customers worldwide. To be competitive, your company must be both international and local in outlook. It must reject the outdated 'global' and 'multinational' models of business and aim to become 'A Global Integrated Enterprise (GIE)' instead.

Forget global, think 'A Global Integrated Enterprise (GIE)'

Everyone hates buzz-terms until they become irreplaceable. So take a moment to mouth the words 'A Global Integrated Enterprise'. To understand where it's come from and why it's necessary, you simply need to look at its predecessors.

First, the 'global' corporation. Highly centralized, this model is shaped like a pyramid where strategy and processes are devised at the top and distributed down a rigid series of management tiers. It used to be popular among US brands, who saturated their domestic markets and then tried to approach foreign markets with cookie-cutter products and services. Take IBM; the undisputed heavyweight of the computer mainframe industry, it saw no reason to believe that customer requirements for its technology could differ all over the world. Surely, it thought, any diverse structures and practices it encountered in strange, foreign lands would eventually bow to the Stars and Stripes, which had become a heraldic symbol for global business convergence. This applied to sales and marketing conventions as much as anything else – keep them close to your chest, the thinking went, and lead by example. It worked well during the 1980s, when the global appetite for mainframes seemed insatiable, then it fell out of fashion quicker than shiny shoulder-pads and ankle-socks. IBM scrabbled to compete with rivals who were suddenly offering localized products by giving its international units more autonomy and, as a result, becoming much more locally focused and flexible.

Next, consider the 'multinational' corporation. Highly devolved as a matter of course, it trusts its international unit to know what's best for their particular territory, and to tailor their strategy and operations optimally as a result. The core doesn't intervene in their affairs all that much – it's little more than a treasury, approving their business plans and ruling on acquisition or divestment opportunities. Phillips, Unilever and Hewlett-Packard exemplified this structure until the early 1990s.

In a multinational, the regional offices usually get their own sub-brands – so, for example, GM set up Vauxhall in the UK and Opel in Germany. This makes sense when you consider that each territory also has its own R&D, manufacturing, marketing and selling functions, intended to optimize customer-focus and market-responsiveness. But it doesn't make sense when you consider the huge overheads duplicated across the world as different parts of the same organization replicate each other's work except for a few cultural tics.

Take the best features of both these structures, stir gently and you end up with a GIE, one that can meet local needs while achieving global economies of scale. To paraphrase the organizational theorist Charles Handy, it is a 'corporate elephant' capable of acting like an 'entrepreneurial flea'.

Again, credit must go to the communications revolution for making this versatility possible. In the past, tiers of middle-managers were used to proliferate a company's vision from the board downwards; now, ICTs enable information to flow up, down and sideways. The results typically include a flattened corporate hierarchy, reduced duplication of efforts, improved market-responsiveness and a more rapid identification and dissemination of best practice. However, the essential quality of the GIE is adaptability: as it becomes less beholden to geography, so it can review its portfolio continuously based on incoming local knowledge, then use the flexible relationships it has formed with suppliers, distributors and other stakeholders to seize opportunities. It can draw upon its global core strengths and constantly reconfigure these to meet changing local market needs.

The world's biggest car-makers have taken some of the biggest steps towards the GIE ideal in recent years[1] – they've had to, because the value of their fixed assets is so high, and because most have large workforces that are heavily protected by unions and advanced employment law. They've harnessed the latest developments in computer-aided design, materials and assembly processes to deliver products for specific territories based on detailed local preferences. Yet they've also found ways to create fresh global efficiencies – GM, for example, announced in November 2005 that its new vehicles would increasingly be localized variations on a handful of 'core global model ranges'. Similarly, pharmaceutical companies are increasingly coordinating their R&D and manufacturing capabilities to tailor products to the varying demands of national regulatory authorities, which often stipulate different criteria for clinical trials, product specification, packaging and post-prescription monitoring.

The lifeblood of this type of effort is information, making the control of information an essential discipline for any aspiring transnational corporation to learn. In other types of company, the role of the chief information officer (CIO) may simply be one of support, covering such things as data management systems, telephone and computer networks or intellectual property rights. In the GIE, they must have a key strategic role, governing the exchange, interpretation and application of data from every source, as well as the ICTs that make such an exchange possible.

Of course, some data only makes sense in its cultural context. So to be a true GIE, a company must learn to manage cultural diversity across its business units, and the relationships this entails. This doesn't mean rejecting the idiosyncrasies, views and business practices of the place where your company was founded, in favour of vanilla thinking. On the contrary, it is the clash of ideas between people in different international units, as well as those with different functions, that is likely to generate creative 'outside the box' thinking and your most valuable innovations. The challenge is to harmonize this diversity, and align it to the vision of the company as a whole. As Western companies become more global in their operations there is a greater need to have senior management teams reflecting cultural diversity. According to Coutts Bank, 92,000 overseas executives arrive in Britain each year engaged on corporate assignments of variable duration.

Here's an idea: why not recruit local specialists to senior management positions in proportion to the size of the growth markets they represent? Many US companies are now doing so, poaching talent from India and China in recognition of the fact that those two countries will soon be its biggest markets. Or consider IBM; it is investing $10 billion dollars in India to create a future R&D talent pool.

Just don't forget that the ultimate responsibility of any manager is to build positive working relationships, whether at the international, interdisciplinary, intercorporate or individual level. No matter what its size, your company is now in the business of establishing a network that will enable it to be as efficient and nimble as possible. But such a network is only strong when each of its nodes shares the same vision. The solution is long-term relationships between corporate cores and small, local partners – by 2020, the practice of offshoring for short-term gain without any regard for long-term integrity will be inexcusable to shareholders and should already be inexcusable to any internationally minded manager. It is long-term deals that will generate the greatest efficiencies and growth opportunities, motivating the most far-flung suppliers and distributors to improve their capabilities in human resources (HR), technology and other areas.

The successful GIE doesn't get hung up on the idea of setting up foreign offices. Why bother when a contracting arrangement or joint venture enables it to remain more adaptable? Yet even in these situations it will rely on its ability to build trust through face-to-face meetings. In the past, the phrase 'people are your greatest asset' was a platitude. Today it needs to be tattooed on the body of every senior manager in the world, but particularly in the West, where talent is in short supply, and dwindling fast.

The ongoing war for talent

The consulting firm McKinsey didn't understate things when, in 1997, it predicted a 'War For Talent' among Western companies. That war is now raging, and is set to get even bloodier as global demographics work to Asia's advantage. By 2020, the proportion of people over 60 will be 25 per cent in Europe, about the same in the UK and 22 per cent in the United States. In the same year, China and India will have comparative figures of 17 and 10 per cent respectively, meaning they'll be less burdened by the elderly and will have a deeper reservoir of young adults from which to draw the capabilities they need. Much deeper, in fact – together, they will continue to account for almost a third of the world's population. What's more, their education systems are improving rapidly, with China developing higher education facilities to rival the best in the world and India consolidating its relatively high proportion of English speakers.

It's enough to make the corporate Western executives hot under their white collars and tunics. How can you possibly hold on to your competitive advantage when Asia is awash with cheap talent, able to compete in even the most complex service industries?

One thing that should help is the recruitment of more expatriates, especially from markets where you expect strong future growth. However, the number of people willing to switch countries for their careers will always be limited. Another defence strategy could be to offshore some of your core competencies – indeed, if most of your company is publicly traded then your shareholders may decide a shift of gravity is in their best interests. However, it is the only realistic option for large companies able to detach themselves completely from their home nation, in terms of its culture, heritage and political environment, as well as its clusters of commercial and research organizations. Usually, it happens only as the result of a merger and even then in a corporate structure where brand-founding offices are preserved.

So let's examine the options at home. They fall broadly into two camps: 1) improved recruitment and retention; and 2) improved leverage of intellectual capital. To achieve either of these you first need to understand what's happening to the average workplace, in terms of its stratification of roles. By 2020, the best GIE companies will consist of five discrete types of personnel.

1. Corporate celebrities – the pin-up ambassadors

The word 'celebrity' has taken on some odd connotations in recent years. It seems to be confused with 'greatness' by the TV-watching public in many countries, thanks to Hollywood and the US movie industry. In the business world, of course, a leader only becomes celebrated if he or she achieves positive results that everybody else can recognize. The consequences of 'eviction' are more serious too – in this context, it means the ruin of your reputation, either through a vote of no-confidence from shareholders, a forced resignation or commercial collapse. Nevertheless, some of the rules of movie stardom are becoming more applicable in the boardroom. Take 'image', for example – the continued proliferation of the mass media means it really is more important to appear professional, competent and self-assured through your appearance and body language.

Essentially, the role of the corporate celebrity is ambassadorial. He or she must consistently embody the core values and culture of the corporation, both externally – lobbying politicians; helping to handle key clients and investors; appearing in the media – and internally – aligning every member of staff to a strategic vision. The importance of the latter can't be overstated: alignment is a vital quality of a GIE because it operates in a variety of countries, employs people from a variety of different cultures and depends on localized products and services coupled with global economies of scale. You don't necessarily need a presidential style of management to align a large company, pressing the palm of every employee on a regular basis. However, to be a true corporate celebrity you do need to be inspiring, continually finding new ways to ensure that everyone in the company shares the same ambition. This is what Branson did at Virgin in the UK in its early days. It is what Jack Welch in the United States did at General Electric (GE) and what every successful entrepreneur takes for granted as the key to business success.

This is an elite cadre in which every member has the Midas touch. It is analogous to the world's 'magic circles' of football players, actors or even politicians. Accordingly, it will always be associated with stratospheric rewards. The pay-gap between corporate celebrities and other types of worker is likely to increase over the coming decades owing to a global shortage of senior executive leadership skills.

Many CEOs have already ignored the advice of management guru Peter Drucker, who suggested that the person on the top rung of any organization should not earn more than 20 times the salary of anyone on the bottom rung. However, as ethical boycotting continues to grow more advanced and influential, their earnings potential may be reined in. At the same time, they will probably hold their leadership positions for shorter periods of time. In the past, the way to become a chief executive was to climb the corporate ladder over a long period of time, displaying deep corporate loyalty. In the future, companies will have to set themselves tighter deadlines to maintain their competitive advantage, and may therefore find that a corporate celebrity, hired on an interim basis, is their best source of experience and expertise for the challenges they are about to face. Increasingly, corporate celebrities will specialize in areas of leadership such as turnarounds or mergers and acquisitions, and operate on fixed-term contracts with specified performance targets. Tomorrow? This practice is already gathering pace today.

2. Corporate lieutenants – lenses and loudhailers

What a leader starts, a manager finishes. It's the job of the 'corporate lieutenant' to realize the vision of the corporate celebrity – refining company policy, formulating business plans for their units, and ensuring the best ideas flow up, down and sideways. The highest concentration of MBA graduates in a company is likely to be situated in this rank of employees – it's where general management skills and best-practice know-how are most in demand. Yet a lieutenant is not merely someone who lacks the inspiration to be a celebrity. He or she is a specialist whose role is indispensable, even if his or her tenure may be subject to increasing risk.

Corporate lieutenants have to motivate and inspire staff at a local level. They must be lenses for the corporate vision. They must also be loudhailers for all the valuable ideas and information their business unit comes across. If their area of responsibility is company-wide, their 'local' knowledge will probably be process or resource based. That is to say, they'll have a uniquely keen awareness of how to optimize their unit's performance, and why this is integral to the performance of the company as a whole. Take the IT director; he or she can probably generate efficiencies faster than anyone else in the modern organization, through the introduction of new software, hardware or ways of doing things. However, it's the heads of market-specific teams who will prove most valuable to the average company in the coming decades. These corporate lieutenants will know their local market inside and out – as such, they'll be crucial to the company's diversification, because the most successful products and services will be those that have local and personal appeal.

Big pressures, big risks, big rewards. Corporate lieutenants will have to be experts in both internal and external benchmarking and quality assurance, because their highly incentivized packages, including significant amounts of equity as well as cash, will depend largely on how their performance compares to specific aims and objectives. They'll have tough targets to meet every quarter (or even more frequently) based on the generation of sales, profits, savings and shareholder value. What's more, they'll face the unique challenge of how to reconcile their company's overall vision with its need to be highly decentralized and disaggregated – in other words, they'll spend a large amount of time coordinating globally distributed units and smoothing over rocky relationships.

One of the main challenges facing corporate celebrities will be how to empower their lieutenants. Every leader goes through a period of delegation anxiety, of course, and this experience will become more acute as the transnational model requires companies to establish mini-fiefdoms in countries all over the world. The more control you give away, the less certainty you have that your vision is being realized in the way you planned. However, there's a new delegation danger that has been created by the networking of the global economy. Today, if a corporate lieutenant feels their employer is too slow to innovate, too cumbersome, too bureaucratic or just too risk-averse, they will find it easier than ever to set up a rival company and become an entrepreneur in their own right. A clear understanding of the rules of intrapreneurship will be needed by companies who wish to keep their best corporate lieutenants in-house.

3. Corporate stalwarts – craftpeople of the knowledge economy

Welcome to the cutting edge of the modern corporation, comprised of lower-level managers and highly specialized full-timers. These 'doers' are essential to your core operations – they are the engineers who maintain IT systems; the chemists, designers and chefs who help you diversify; the production managers who model, assemble and pack your products; and many others whose roles are minor in isolation but vital in aggregate.

Expertise at this level is based on execution: while lieutenants convert vision into policy, these men and women convert policy into process. They tend to be grouped in silos of talent, each with its own identity, culture and even sub-brand. Meanwhile, remuneration is based largely on the scarcity value of each stalwart's skills. Each will have performance-related incentives to aim for, but they will have less exposure to risk than their lieutenants, in line with their lower pay packets. Unless their entire company or industry is threatened, they can expect to be in demand continuously – provided they develop their own skills and talents continuously too.

No stalwart can assume that the knowledge they have today will be enough to keep them in employment tomorrow. During the Industrial Revolution (and for some time after), they would have performed one repetitive task until they were sacked, retired, retrained or mutilated by dangerous machinery. In the knowledge economy, they need to acquire new skills throughout their working lives to maintain their own competitive advantage and, by extension, that of their companies. Certain jobs may look as if they involve the same skills, processes and duties as they did a year ago, or even a decade ago. However, most have evolved beyond recognition from the perspective of the stalwart. The applied benefit may be the same, but you can bet that today's customers expect it to be achieved much faster and more efficiently than those of the past. Accordingly, a stalwart must keep abreast of the latest tools of their trade and the networked communication skills required to ensure they are deployed efficiently.

Take telephone engineers, for example. In the past, they would have spent most of their time up telegraph poles or wiring extension sockets. Today, they must understand how to make repairs remotely through digital exchanges, and how to integrate the voice services with a variety of new home-entertainment and home business applications such as broadband internet access and cable TV. If they're part of a large corporation – whether an infrastructure and service provider such as BT, France Telecom or BellSouth or an outsourced support services agency – they'll probably also need to master a handheld unit that tells their lieutenant when a job is complete, plus the satellite navigation system that enabled them to find the end-user in the first place.

Even in the service industries, the bar has been raised in terms of minimal skills and capabilities: 50 years ago, an investment banker would have used blackboards and stationery to make presentations; 25 years ago it was whiteboards and overhead projectors. Today it's *PowerPoint*, the presentation software application produced by Microsoft. Yet we're already seeing the cracks appearing in the dominance of the computer-based presentation, with its animated graphics, sound effects and tendency to overwhelm the viewer. As it has become ubiquitous, so it has become less surprising and arguably less impressive in, say, sales situations. A growing number of businesspeople are paying specialized consultants to train up their sales and interpersonal skills from the perspective of vocal projection, speech-writing and body language. They are looking for a new differentiator to give them competitive advantage, in the same way that Darwin's hawkmoth needed a 10-inch proboscis to feed off the Madagascar orchid.[2]

As the changing nature of most industries continues to accelerate, so it will become more important for human resources to be rapidly re-deployable. It is therefore in the interests of companies to ensure that their stalwarts are given sufficient training and sufficient time in which to study and hone their skills. At the same time, companies must exploit the proximity of their stalwarts to customers and encourage them to disseminate information about, say, aesthetic preferences or backfiring functionality up the chain of command. In the 21st century, 360° feedback will be one of the best sources of innovation.

4. Corporate travellers – the footloose freelances

Yesterday's companies were built brick by brick from the ground up, tomorrow's will flow like streams on shifting sands adapting continuously to new threats and opportunities. Its temporary workers will allow them to achieve this structure, with greater speed and efficiency than is possible today. They'll increasingly be recruited at short notice, for short periods to meet short-term needs. The growth of outsourcing over the past 30 years is part of a long-term trend towards a 'stock market' of human resources, on which individuals will auction their services to the highest bidder.

To be a corporate traveller, you need to be empowered, to some extent by your employment rights but mainly by your curriculum vitae. In countries like China, temporary workers will continue to be hired and fired en masse until their employment rights improve. The only exceptions to this rule will be the children of the new urban elite, many of whom are already being educated abroad, who will be able to demonstrate their value to foreign companies unilaterally. The rise of the freelance is already becoming well established. It combines the specialist

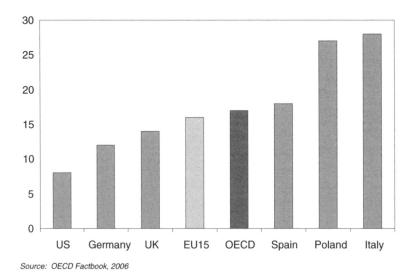

Source: *OECD Factbook, 2006*

Figure 2.1 Self-employment rates across selected countries (% of all total civilian employment)

knowledge of the stalwart with the breadth of experience from a variety of different employing corporations. By far the most visible type of corporate traveller is the consultant, whether in strategic management, international finance or law. The category also includes the elite members of the creative industries, such as web design, advertising and filmmaking.

While corporate lieutenants are loyal, corporate travellers are opportunist. They don't want to stay long-term at a company unless they are given interesting work or more money than they can earn elsewhere. This attitude can act like a breath of fresh air: if a freelance joins you out of genuine interest for your line of work then the chances are they will complete their contract enthusiastically, and energize the full-time staff they meet along the way. On the other hand, their loyalty is not guaranteed, and employers who use them in large numbers need to be aware that this can leave the company vulnerable in certain areas. Quality assurance, for example, becomes more difficult when you have a continuous stream of newcomers working on the same products and services. More importantly, you need to ensure you have security systems that protect you against the leaking of intellectual property or other commercially sensitive information.

Ultimately, corporate travellers enable companies to engage in 'asymmetric warfare' with their rivals. Provided they are managed correctly, they can be deployed in any size or shape, in any place, at high speed, to direct your brand, resources and know-how where they can derive the most value. You can see this principle working vividly in the film industry, where tiny production companies are formed and re-formed all the time to manage specific projects. Sadly, you can also see it in the operations of terrorist organizations such as Al-Qaeda. The latter example is salutary in that it demonstrates how an overarching vision can be used to inspire disparate units to the same end. Adopting such tactics for peaceful and mutually rewarding ends is one of the best ways businesspeople can create opportunities in developing countries and, with them, compelling alternatives to fatalist extremism.

5. Corporate orphans – the outsiders looking in

The further you get from the source of your income, the more likely you are to be a corporate orphan. If you're a factory seamstress in China, a fruit-picker in Spain, a coffee-grower in Colombia or even an assembly technician on a production line in the United States then you are probably at the mercy of one or two clients, somewhere further up the supply chain. If they suffer then you suffer exponentially more – it's that simple.

Like the travellers, the corporate orphans are the product of increased outsourcing and offshoring. But they have fewer options. In areas where globalization has been most abused, workers in this category are subject to *de facto* bondage, unable to free themselves from a poverty cycle of their employer's creation. Thankfully, globalization has also had the opposite effect, lifting them off the breadline and giving them hope for the future. Nevertheless, the dependants are financially restricted and exposed to major swings of fortune. The GIE is one that can and must reshuffle its supply chain at a moment's notice; the negative impact of this flexibility is the human cost when impoverished communities lose major contracts. And when a corporate celebrity never sees your face, it's hard to engage his or her sympathy. It's the responsibility of governments to ensure that these workers are given a good standard of basic education and as many transferable skills as possible, to provide a safety net for the most vulnerable people in their society while maintaining the flexibility in their labour markets to attract the companies that will improve the prosperity of the country as a whole. But it will be the obligation of companies to ensure that such rights are being granted to offshore employees, as corporate social responsibility becomes more important to customers and shareholders, and to the integrity and sustainability of brands.

Hold tight and harmonize

With such disparate types of worker, spread widely and reshuffled constantly, how can you possibly find a reward structure to attract the best people, bring out their best and keep them aligned to a common goal? The solution depends largely on how far each of their countries has risen up Maslow's 'hierarchy of needs'. In the developing world, the priority of unskilled workers is clearly the money they need to improve their quality of life and that of their families; in the developed world, the incentivizing power of money is diminishing. Today, if you want to recruit and retain the best Western talent, you need be creative, finding ways to offer psychological as well as material well-being.

Personal freedom is at number one on the wish-list of most knowledge workers. In terms of working hours, they want flexibility, increased maternity and paternity leave, maybe sabbaticals for personal development. In terms of personal space, they want offices they can personalize and processes that they can mould around their own lifestyles. In terms of intrapreneurship, they want to be able to lead a project as if it were a company in its own right, with co-ownership of intellectual property rights and share options in any resulting spin-off ventures.

Another growing consideration, particularly for jobseekers, is the company's brand – would talented young recruits really want to associate themselves with someone of your reputation? Western young people are more willing than ever to boycott products based on their perception of a brand's ethics. They're more able too – thanks ironically to the consumer choice, net-worked technologies and affluent comfort of the system many claim to hate. Clearly, no business in its right mind would recruit people who throw bricks at McDonald's on May Day. Nevertheless, you do have to acknowledge that there is a growing link between your ethical stance and your ability to pick and choose the best workers. This trend isn't confined to obvious sins such as sweatshop labour and pollution; it also encompasses sus-tainability in all its forms, family-friendly policies and links with local communities. What's more, for those already on your payroll, the brand is crucial to an individual's identity with the whole, and becoming more so as the transnational ideal leads increasingly to the disaggregation of business units across the world. It is one of the chief responsibilities of corporate celebrities – arguably the most important – to preserve and continuously improve the reputation of their corporate brands. The status of the leader and their company flag is generally mutually reinforc-ing or mutually destructive.

Of course, a brand doesn't only communicate values. It also sug-gests to employees what a company might be like to work for. Does your brand connote excitement thanks to its creativity and non-conformism? If not, you can bet tomorrow's top-performing stu-dents will put your details somewhere near the bottom of the pile of prospectuses they receive when blue-chip firms visit their uni-versity for the annual courting season. In the UK, this is known as the 'Milk Round', because it used to be an easy method of extract-ing the best product from the best universities. Today, the term is a misnomer, because skills shortages have created competition among employers – they now vie for the attention of undergradu-ates with a variety of immediate incentives, principally free bars and buffets. Tomorrow, the process will be almost fully inverted: it will be the holders of the intellectual assets rather than the holders of the paychecks who will wield the most power.

You might think it's impossible to guarantee excitement, creative duties and a non-conformist attitude at your company because it has grown too large. If so, you need to start working out how to break down your internal structures. Many companies have already realized the benefits of creating entrepreneurial cells internally. These not only make it easier to recruit the best talent, on account of their dynamism and 'collegiate' branding, but also enable the company as a whole to be more innovative and responsive to threats and opportunities (see below). Jack Welch, the former CEO of GE, has for many years encouraged other business leaders to break up business units as soon as they grow to more than 50 people in number. In any case, corporate structures are fragmenting naturally as a consequence of the rapid changes occurring in most industries. In most Western companies, competitive advantage is now derived largely from project-based initiatives. As a result, workers tend to identify first with the project team around them and latterly with their company as a whole. This disparity will become greater and potentially more disruptive, leading to corporate anarchy unless companies learn how to manage it – again, a matter of alignment for which the corporate celebrity is ultimately responsible.

Don't be fooled into thinking that you can rely on the internet or some other networking technology to keep your project teams together. Until you can shake hands with someone inside a virtual reality chamber, this will remain nothing more than a fantasy for IT consultants. Regular face-to-face contact has always been vital for the development of trust and the efficient exchange of ideas between team members, and will continue to be so for the foreseeable future. Indeed, a paradox of the wired world and the e-corporation is that the nurturing of human relations and the psychological contract with employees have become more, rather than less, important.

If your workplace isn't a sociable place then its competitive advantage is rapidly and invisibly dying. Office chat is a vastly underrated source of new ideas, of the sort that will be crucial to the diversification of the future corporation. Research on high-performing technology companies confirms this. What's more, your rivals will find it more difficult to imitate your working practices the more they are built on intense personal relationships. It's not for no reason that modern office architecture and facilities management are geared towards face-to-face communication, with coffee machines installed in the middle of work areas so that people bump into each other, and executive offices located in places where colleagues can drop in on an informal and frequent basis. That is why new corporate buildings incorporate numerous coffee areas and attractive restaurant facilities. These encourage collective sociability and through this the flow of creative ideas and product innovation. The working lunch is back with a vengeance and with it the end of the lunch break. Take a look at Telenor's building in Oslo, Norway, for an outstanding example of inspirational architecture geared towards sociability, creativity and innovation.

Across the huge pharmaceutical firm GlaxoSmithKline, staff restaurants are widely regarded as crucial to the discovery and development of new drugs. They serve good-quality food in an environment that encourages socializing – as a result, scientists gather there and take the time to think about and discuss their work, rather than feeling pressured to eat sandwiches in the laboratory or at their desks. Undoubtedly, ideas generated here have improved the company's bottom line. Yet there is another way to loosely quantify the value of the place – if staff are using the time they spend there to, effectively, do more work and carry out meetings, then they work fewer billable hours and complete tasks faster. The moral of the story for any company is that denying social occasions and 'chill-out zones' on the grounds of cost or flippancy is a totally false economy.

Similarly, corporate get-togethers, which have been much maligned in recent years, have a unique potential to bond workers and set out an inspirational agenda for the future, while simultaneously making everyone feel good about themselves and their brand. It is rather like going to church to reaffirm shared beliefs and identities. Despite recent periods of economic downturn, companies have been reluctant to cut annual celebrations from the budget; on the contrary, they have been spending more than ever on events that are bigger, grander and more exotic. For example, France Telecom hired the entire Disneyland Paris resort in 2003 to entertain its 40,000 employees and their families. By contrast, the UK luxury speedboat manufacturer Sunseeker chose exclusivity over scale when, in 2002, it took its network of international dealers to a Finnish hotel inside the Arctic Circle – the 500 attendees got fantastic off-piste skiing in beautiful surroundings and the chance to see the Northern Lights. Such experiences are the logical extension of a principle that has always been popular in corporate bonding efforts – get your people to engage in some kind of emotionally or physically intense activity (preferably both) and they will establish a common identity, becoming even more motivated and inspired. This is why small but exciting activities such as sailing, canoeing and white-water rafting have, for several decades now, been popular destinations for teams whose performance has dropped. US companies give key priority to mega-events, sustaining through them a multi-billion-dollar corporate entertainment/ event marketplace. These are not only major sources of revenue for business gurus but also ex-presidents and prime ministers.

Back at the office, location is perhaps the deciding factor in recruitment and retention. If your staff can walk outside and stroll among the parks, boutiques and bars of a nice part of town, then you will accrue two benefits: 1) casual enterprise of the sort described found at the Glaxo restaurant above and 2) an active desire to be a part of your firm from young recruits who want proximity to the best possible amenities so they don't feel they are wasting the best years of their lives. Most industry clusters are not engineered by governments through tax incentives, they are the result of talented people gathering in attractive places, then setting up similar companies until it becomes unthinkable for rivals to set up elsewhere. This is why the global entertainment industry still centres on Los Angeles, why fashion still begins and ends in Paris and why any self-respecting advertising agency still needs a presence in New York and/or London. Your company may not need to be part of an industry cluster to perform well, but it certainly needs to offer easy access to a high-quality lifestyle.[3]

Corporate creativity: why it takes more than beanbags and Frappuccino

In the past, the term 'workplace' meant just that: a place where work was done, and little else. Today, it's a place where ideas are exchanged and problems are solved. In the best companies, it's also a place where staff feel comfortable enough to socialize and, as a result, better able to carry out their duties.

Note I said 'exchanged' just then instead of 'generated'. The fact is, while many valuable ideas are generated inside offices, factories and laboratories, an equal number are generated in bars, studies and bathtubs. This is why executives shouldn't delude themselves into thinking they can foist creativity onto their employees like some kind of dress-down directive. Yes, idea-generation is becoming ever more important to companies the world over. But it's not a business function in itself. Generally, it's the side-effect of a certain type of corporate culture. You can't legislate for it, *per se*. What you can and should do is ensure that your staff have their imagination stimulated, acknowledged and appropriately rewarded.

Admittedly, it's easier to build this kind of environment in some industries than in others. In bioscience, for example, many companies already offer their staff a stakeholder interest in any ideas they generate that go on to be successfully commercialized. This not only helps them to develop new products and services but also to prevent staff from leaving to become entrepreneurs, taking their best ideas with them. By contrast, in the entertainment industry, recognition is the principal spur to innovation, and is becoming available in an increasing number of flavours. Consider the production staff on feature films, for example. They used to be invisible to the public, even if their name could be glimpsed briefly when the credits rolled. Today, the best star in 'Making of...' documentaries and behind-the-scenes footage (increasingly available as DVD extras). As a result, their profile is raised – if they were corporate stalwarts before then they are likely to become corporate travellers soon after, or be granted new powers and rewards from their existing employer.

Your organization doesn't have to operate at the cutting edge of science or entertainment to benefit or suffer from these trends. Many companies already have initiatives in place to reward employees, no matter what their rank, for generating ideas that have an impact on the bottom line. Indeed, good ideas are likely to flow more often from front-line members of staff in the coming decades because they are more likely to deal with customers, get their hands dirty with processes handed down from on high and learn more than anybody else in their organizations about local markets. Equally, a variety of companies are benefiting from the desire for recognition via weblogs. Blogging enables individuals who would previously have been invisible to raise their profile throughout their organizations or industries. The benefits for employers who permit employees to blog using their systems include the improved dissemination of best-practice information, and in some cases a safeguard against duplication of research and development. The drawbacks include an increased vulnerability to headhunting and quandaries over censorship.

The essential point for company bosses to remember, particularly if they are based in the West, is that they must make innovation the business of every employee. In the coming years, it will have the same status that quality assurance had in the 1990s – a distributed process and a collective responsibility. At the same time, the creative corporation can't innovate in all directions. It must focus on ideas that generate genuine value. True, Western companies will have to reinvent themselves more frequently in future, with a shifting portfolio that responds to consumer needs, but to endure they must also consolidate what they do best.

Most companies have a lifespan of only a few years. Many others have internal processes that are insufficient to keep up with external trends. For most of them, positive change is likely to take the form of a merger or an acquisition – indicators that one of the parties lacks vision or strategic foresight; employs the wrong performance indicators and benchmarks; or has left it too late to unravel their culture of complacency. Companies with more longevity have a very clear understanding of their core markets, while also having the ability to imagine new ones. Ever heard of the Beatles? They endured not because they became a different band with each album but because they pushed their creativity as far as possible while remaining recognizable as John, Paul, Ringo and George. The same principle applies to Madonna – she has succeeded through continuous reinvention while most other music business celebrities pass through like ships in the night.

Companies that wish to thrive beyond 2020 need a very particular kind of creativity: one that creates platforms from which they can continuously develop new products and services for changing market needs. They need to be able to build scenarios – gathering high-quality information about customer tastes, then subjecting it to intelligent interpretation. Nokia, the Finnish mobile phone manufacturer, began life in 1865 as a wood-pulp mill. During the 1990s, it had envisaged a world characterized by mobility, in which people regarded boundless communication as essential to their social life as well as their professional life. Since then, it has taken on some of the world's giant electronics companies and won itself a 35 per cent share of the mobile market, while doing more than any other company to accessorize the mobile phone. Similarly, when Apple Computer launched the iPod in 2001, it seemed an unnatural step for a company with no experience of producing portable music players. In fact, it was a runaway success that catalysed an entirely new industry – the retailing of music and other entertainment content online.[4]

Despite numerous case studies like this, most large companies continue to believe that the most lucrative innovations will emerge from their core competencies. It's an understandable instinct – trying to use what you do best to create something new – but in the business world it's generally misguided. The problem is, you can only sell so many refinements to your core product lines before you overshoot what most consumers need or are willing to digest. Fail to consider wholly different ways of doing things and you leave yourself vulnerable to smaller rivals who can move faster and are willing to settle for lower margins. Recent research from South Korea, carried out by a team including Professor Dylan Jones-Evans, showed that of 120 companies classified 'most innovative' by the government, the most successful were those that tried to learn continually from their competitors and other external sources of information about their markets.

Many large organizations have another bad habit: they try so hard to read customers that they become reactive rather than proactive in the way they innovate. Consider Sony in the years between the peak of the Walkman's success and the launch of its PlayStation games console – it knew lots about the people who bought its products but nothing about the people who came into its stores and bought nothing, nor about how its core market was evolving in terms of lifestyle. The same was the case with the British retailer, Marks & Spencer. Sony had great information management systems in place, but what it needed was a culture that placed employee imagination over the supposed infallibility of technology. Lest we forget, it is the 'software culture' still widespread in many industries today that has created rigid processes of the sort we all suffer from when dealing with call centres.

To thrive and survive, you want to be close enough to your customer to sense incipient trends, but detached enough to marshal your R&D, marketing and sales operations accordingly. You also need to collaborate with your business partners to collect and share data, and to ensure your supply chain is ready to handle new sources of demand as they are identified. Customer intelligence, as opposed to mere customer knowledge, is now an essential corporate capability.

Weird, extrovert, non-conformist: meet your ideal employee

As the value of brainpower continues to outstrip that of fixed assets, so organizations all over the world, and especially in the West, must spend more time fostering positive and stimulating personal relationships between employees. Your staff may come to work because they love the vision and brand created by your corporate celebrity, but they won't stay unless they get along with their colleagues in the kind of informal, flexible and playful environment that the best innovations require (or unless you bribe them, which is a more expensive and less effective basis for innovation). The problem with most corporate bonding or culture-building events is that they encourage compliance and conformity, creating superficial relationships and linear thinking. Even the sexiest brand will see its creative streak wither and die if its staff are told constantly to follow 'the corporate way of doing things'. This is what IBM did in the early 1990s.

What an ideas-based business needs are employees who are individualistic, non-conformist, challenging and questioning, as well as willing to accept and deliver positive criticism. More importantly, the organization needs to be tolerant of such a human melting pot, and prepared to make the extra effort to manage its inevitable clashes. Creating such a culture often demands a change in recruitment practices. Too many businesses hire people on the basis that they will 'fit in' (who will, in other words, conform to and comply with the status quo). Many reject CVs that indicate numerous career changes, fearing this indicates personal 'instability'. Yet we know that today's young professionals, especially those in the West, value personal freedoms above all else, and aspire to experiences as much as material goods. In such a context, frequent job shifts could suggest valuable traits: their independence, for example, could be the result of a high-quality education and diligent study, while they will undoubtedly have benefited from the experience of a wide range of work environments. The problem for many companies is that they want to have creative, innovative corporate cultures but are reluctant to take the self-confident risks and recruit people who have exactly the personal attributes needed to bring this about.

It follows that job descriptions in many organizations also need to change radically. In the past, they were defined clearly in terms of pay and responsibility – indeed, the principle of 'instrumental compliance', under which manufacturers use pay as their primary source of motivation. Such an arrangement is totally irrelevant for the knowledge-based businesses of today, where flexibility is more important than stability. Yet its passing creates problems: for example, if the most creative employees are also the most independent, how is it possible to get them cooperating with others and aligning with the goals of the corporation, rather than regarding the company simply as a resource pool for personal gain? There is no definitive answer to this question: it's a reality that certain industries such as the media have simply learnt to ameliorate or accommodate.

A related issue is that when creatives develop an affinity to a team, it is often because they believe they can use the skills of their colleagues to their own ends or because they enjoy working with others with similar personalities. This often creates counter-cultures within organizations that breed cynicism or resentment, because allegiance is to immediate teams or bosses and not to the ultimate employer. Taken to the extreme, it leads to corporate fragmentation. Many media companies are held together solely by a few positive brand values and the monthly salary cheque, but it's also often a feature of universities, hospitals and other knowledge-based businesses where intellectual capital is the operating core. The loosening of management processes thus raises difficult questions. Where does the responsibility of one individual or team begin and end? How much authority can a middle-manager exercise without referral to higher levels? And, most fundamental of all, does strategy necessarily need to permeate from the top down if the business is based on imagination and foresight?

To resolve these issues, a company needs a strong brand and a strong corporate celebrity with an inspiring and unifying vision. It needs to develop a trust culture and discretionary management practices, so that staff have greater operational autonomy, authority and responsibility, with concomitant performance-appraisal schemes and reward systems. It also needs to expose teams and individuals to greater target-setting, benchmarking and accountability. A paradox of the knowledge-based business is that with greater freedom come tighter controls. This obviously creates new problems – witness the resentment among teachers, academics, medics, social workers and many others whose outputs are now subject to performance reviews, and the constant protest over the reliability and validity of these measures being used to assess performance and apportion rewards – but it is absolutely essential if resources are not to be wasted. By 2020, the best-practice management model will resemble a professional practice such as a university, but it won't permit the same lack of direction and focus.[5]

Leading companies in industries such as pharmaceuticals, the media and software are already building a collegiate structure in which processes are structured around time and cost budgets, and negotiated between team leaders and senior management, with interference from above occurring only at progress reviews. Yet there is, at present, a limit to the number of additional companies that can support such a structure in that we currently have a surplus of managers and a shortage of leaders worldwide. If you want a pervasive culture of trust in which bosses are willing to delegate projects readily to their subordinates, you need people at every level who are inspirational, not simply hands-on, with the emotional, social and technical skills to take self-confident decisions within parameters set by their colleagues and team leaders. In short, you need intrapreneurial vassals, willing to swear allegiance to the monarchical CEO while getting the best out of their own territories. The transition to such a structure is going to be much harder for public companies than it is for private ones – another reason why the current private-equity boom has a long way to go.

Endnotes

1 The UK retailer Tesco is a quintessential cross-border company: a juggernaut in its home country where it accounts for £1 in every £8 of overall retail sales, yet sensitive to local preferences in the regions of its domestic markets, and in 13 other countries worldwide. Its international expansion has been aimed mainly at developing markets with weak incumbent retailers in Central Europe and the Far East. Here it has used joint ventures, for example with Samsung Group in South Korea, to localize its formidable logistical expertise. It appoints a very high proportion of local personnel to management positions. It also continues to be a pioneer in data-mining, using initiatives such as customer loyalty cards to further localize product ranges. About 20 per cent of Tesco's £34 billion turnover in

the year ended February 2005 was made overseas, and the company plans to increase this to 50 per cent in the medium term.

2 Running to stand still: Sticking with evolutionary theory for a moment, it's important for employers to recognize that any training regime they set up for staff is subject to the so-called 'Red Queen Effect', which basically says that in any competitive system you need to 'run in order to stand still', just like the eponymous character from Through the Looking Glass, the sequel to Alice's Adventures in Wonderland, by Lewis Carroll. By the time you've raised the know-how of your staff to best-practice levels, a rival firm somewhere will already have surpassed your efforts. You therefore need to develop your people continuously and, as far as possible, proactively, based on predictions about the future of your industry.

3 Lifestyle leaders: SAS Institute is one of the world's biggest software firms. It develops statistical analysis, data-mining and benchmarking software for other large organizations – not the most sexy job description in the world – but has a staff turnover far lower than the industry average. Why? Because it puts huge efforts into generating job satisfaction among its employees, and not only through competitive salaries. Staff are trained continuously and to a high quality; they have access to the best equipment – an appealing feature for any engineer; and they are forbidden from working after 6 pm. What's more, SAS facilities are based almost exclusively in picturesque surroundings – in the UK, for example, the company occupies a stately home on the Thames in rural Buckinghamshire, surrounded by huge grounds, where staff go running and mountain-biking at lunchtime. The US headquarters in Cary, North Carolina, is a campus with its own sports, medical and educational facilities. SAS has frequently been voted among the best places to work in America by its employees, while performing well commercially.

4 Think opportunities, not resources: The development of the iPod exemplifies what Harvard professor Clayton Christensen calls the 'jobs to be done' approach to innovation. Instead of creating another variation on its established product lines, Apple used its capabilities to address the problem of how to store, transport and organize music more conveniently. In other words, it searched for an adverse circumstance that it could solve on the consumer's behalf – a job to be done – rather than searching for ideas within its existing resources.

Professor Clark Gilbert, a colleague of Christensen's both at Harvard and his innovation consultancy Innosight, suggests that large companies should imagine their core competencies as the largest circle in a Venn diagram. The most successful intrapreneurial ventures, he says, begin outside this circle but grow to overlap it, as the iPod has done by becoming an integral part of Apple's holistic view of home entertainment, centred around its Macintosh computer range.

5 The rise of the science park: In fairness to universities, they are becoming much more effective at developing commercially viable technologies. Research carried out on behalf of the UK Science Park Association, for example, shows an increase in total licensing income from £31.3 million in 2003 to £40 million in 2004, with the number of licence agreements more than doubling during this period. But European universities have much to learn from their US counterparts – they have been more entrepreneurial, with more rapid 'ideas-to-market' product cycles.

3 Hunting, farming and fulfilling future talent

Unlimited opportunities or tied to the workplace?

- 'Upside down' reward systems
- Do education systems deliver what companies want?
- Goodbye to the corporate elephants, good day to the corporate fleas
- Why all that wasted talent among women and ethnic minorities?
- Intellectual intelligence – good for college exams but not enough for the job
- Beyond doing the job just for money

There have always been two main categories of worker in the world. Before industrial society, the division was between the people who owned the land and the people who worked it. During the 19th and 20th centuries, it was between the blue-collar manual labourers and the white-collar thinkers. Today, and in the future, it is between the knowledge-workers and those who look after them. In other words, some now have jobs that can be done anywhere while others are tied to specific locations. If you're a software engineer in the United States or Europe you may be afraid of losing your job to someone in India, but plumbers can be fairly secure in the belief that they will always be needed.

Admittedly, this simplified view has its caveats – for example, anyone providing professional services such as legal or financial advice could be classified as both a knowledge-worker and a support service provider, because most of us still prefer to have face-to-face meetings with those we retain for these important matters. Nevertheless, it is certain that knowledge-work will entail greater risks in the future without, necessarily, corresponding gains in its rewards. At the same time, the West will see a resurgence in artisanship, as growing numbers recognize that skilled manual labour cannot easily be offshored.

It's one of the greatest ironies in the history of capitalism: the less well paid jobs of the 19th century are destined to be among the most highly rewarded in the 21st. We are witnessing a resurgence of a craft-based aristocracy, echoing a time prior to the Industrial Revolution when artisans had the highest status. Of course, those with the least skills will continue to earn relatively little – in the West, such workers will end up in so-called 'McJobs', such as fast-food service, check-out operations or cleaning. Yet they should at least find that work is plentiful around successful clusters of knowledge-based companies. And if their governments are sensible then they should also have access to high-quality training and education. By contrast, in India and China, the unskilled will see their pay fluctuate as regional clusters blossom or wither – there have been significant wage rises recently in parts of China's Guangdong province, an industrial heartland, where the flood of cheap migrant labour has finally become a trickle but, for most corporate dependants in Asia, improvements to social services and education can't come soon enough.

In the West, public sectors are growing fast. In most countries they account for between 30 and 40 per cent of all employment. This is not only the result of detailed social policy of the sort promoted by the interventionist European Union. As we'll discuss in Chapter 5, it's also the result of demographic pressures: the ageing of the population, the growth of single-person households, and the general breakdown of family and community networks, which used to provide much of the unpaid support now encumbering state services.

But the education systems of many Western countries still seem to be stuck in the past. As many employers have complained in recent years, schools and universities are failing to equip young people with so-called 'employable skills'. The meaning of this term differs from company to company, but in essence what they're saying is: 'A philosophy graduate may have a sharply honed sense of critical reasoning, but they're of no use to me if they can't be punctual, diligent and reliable.' (In the same breath, they may well add: 'I'd like them to show a little more creativity too.') In the past, a degree needed to provide very little practical 'added value' – it represented brainpower to some extent; it represented a level of attainment in research and project-work; and, depending on the grade of degree, it represented an ability to form arguments and the regurgitation of facts under pressure. Most companies would be willing to spend time and money channelling these qualities into a work function that created an impression on their bottom line.

No longer. As the business world continues to move faster, so more companies will need and expect the young people they recruit to hit the ground running. The problem for Western employers is that, as their margins rely increasingly on specialized products and services, so the generic courses taught at most schools and universities provide fewer relevant skills. What's more, state education in the West is biased towards academic qualifications, under the misapprehension that most of the young people coming through their doors are guaranteed to end up in steady white-collar jobs.

To some extent, the gap between the West's education systems and the requirements of its major employers – with the possible exception of the United States – can be bridged by closer partnerships between companies and educational establishments. These already exist to a greater extent in the United States than in Europe. However, if young people in the West are to benefit fully from the rise of India and China, their education will have to be founded on a wholly different set of attitudes. Yes, vocations must be celebrated rather than belittled but, more funda-mentally, young people must be clear that the highest rewards in the coming decades will go to those whose skill-sets are special-ized enough to be competitive while broad enough to form a viable customer-base. Whether they work for cross-border com-panies or start their own businesses, they will need to deal with multiple nationalities, cultures and time zones. They will also need to develop the social and emotional intelligence to thrive in a project-based environment, while turning their empathy for the customer-base into valuable innovations. A prodigious work ethic will, of course, come in handy too, but even that must be redefined in the West, if its school-leavers and graduates are to compete with their diligent and hungry counterparts in Asia.

Above all, the education systems of the West must stop their implicit division of the workforce into people who make things (products) and people who carry out specialized knowledge-based tasks. Except in the primary industries that supply us with raw materials, we are approaching a point where everyone effectively works in the latter. Why? Because the reasons for keeping manufacturing in-house are rapidly diminishing, and without production at its core, a company is simply a focus for ideas and administration. Even the manufacturers themselves, whose business model will rely on contract-work for multiple cross-border companies, are having their identities superseded by those of the brands stamped on the goods they produce – try disassembling any complex piece of electronics; you'll find it very difficult to determine who the 'original equipment manu-facturers' (OEMs) of each piece (or even of the whole thing) actually are.[1]

A generic education that ended in a degree qualification used to guarantee a secure middle-management position. Today the West needs a diminishing number of middle-managers as large compa-nies flatten their hierarchies. To prosper in the coming decades, young people must be trained to think like entrepreneurs, either to sell themselves and their ideas within transnational corpora-tions, where intrapreneurial cells will become increasingly vital, or alternatively to join, run and start up small businesses which will account for a higher proportion of businesses than ever before.

Welcome to the age of the entrepreneur

Small and medium-sized companies already generate about a third of all new jobs in the West. It's a proportion that's likely to grow in line with demand for services that are more specialized, localized, personalized and highly targeted. The ability to meet focused customer needs has always given small firms a competitive advantage over their larger rivals. And as communications of all types continue to improve, so small companies will be able to devote more resources to their efforts to remain 'close to the customer'. Many are already finding that they are uniquely positioned to act as 'consolidators' of products and services, integrating a range of diverse activities to meet the rarefied needs of highly lucrative clients.

Establishing a business no longer means worrying about vast capital investments in plant or premises – all you really need is a desk, a telephone, some headed paper for invoicing clients and an internet-ready computer. In the knowledge economy, it's easier to act upon ideas and cheaper to write off failures. Other key factors that will contribute to the coming start-up boom are: the increased demand among young professionals in the West for products and services that enable them to express their individuality; the growing ease with which hungry young entrepreneurs in the East can attach themselves to global supply chains, thanks to advances in communications technology and market liberalization; and the increased use of temporary staff among transnational corporations. Many corporate celebrities and corporate travellers will find it beneficial to incorporate themselves or hire employees to whom they can delegate repetitive, low-level tasks, while even corporate orphans in countries with sufficient social mobility could have the opportunity to work for themselves, provided they come up with the right ideas.

Corporate disaffection will also continue to spawn entrepreneurs. It has been doing so for several decades, as the value of knowledge has outstripped that of physical assets. In the high-tech and media industries in particular, staff turnover has been particularly high, as its idea-generators have realized that they can earn substantially more by working outside the constraints of big companies. Take the computer disk drive industry, for example – between 1977 and 1997, around 25 per cent of all new businesses were started by individuals leaving larger firms.[2] These kinds of trends are going to become more pronounced in the coming decades as organizational structures become more fluid. Why should any talented young professional work for a big company when, by starting up a company of their own, they can control their own destiny and potentially earn more money?

The backlash against conformity is growing – in particular, against the conformity created by the most successful corporations of the 20th century. The young professional of today wants to be distinguished as an individual: by their material possessions, by their experiences and by their career choices. For a growing number, this Holy Grail is incompatible with work in a large organization. One of the main challenges facing large companies of tomorrow is how to attract people who actively resist their way of thinking. Certainly, you won't be able to sustain your growth if your best potential recruits think you're intolerant of non-conformity and 'thinking outside the box' – not when your rivals are living up to those attitudes in exciting ways. Even so, too many companies still treat their staff as an operating cost instead of a capital investment. It's a problem that can only be solved through high-quality leadership that isn't afraid of a pervasive entrepreneurial mentality.

Have you forgotten why working for a small company can be so appealing? Perhaps you think it's a 'young person's game' because of the extra energy it requires. If so, you must start looking at your own company through the eyes of a young professional who is just beginning their career – a career in which they are resigned to the prospect of working at half a dozen jobs or more. A small company is more likely to offer them greater autonomy and greater responsibility at much greater speed. It's also more likely to have a culture that is *fit, fresh and fun*.

Why *fit*? Because in a small company you're always having to benchmark, to invest in training and new technologies, to be 'leading edge', to be acutely aware of your competitors. Why *fresh*? Because in a small company you have to change constantly, to innovate, to adapt what you're producing based on customer feedback, to create an environment in which you're continuously coming up with new ideas. Why *fun*? Because you're less likely to come up with those ideas and find the commitment to realize them unless you actually enjoy what you're doing and whom you're doing it with. In a small company, it's easier to find harmony.

Ask yourself: why do most small businesses fail to grow into medium-sized ones (that is, beyond 50 employees)? It's because of the onerous nature of running a medium-sized or large business, with their management-heavy, bureaucratic structures. But not always; Jack Welch managed to avoid it at GE and so, too, does the global integrated company 3M. Larger companies are subject to extra regulation too – whether in terms of health and safety provisions, financial reporting or hiring and firing. Many entrepreneurs complain that, once a business hits a headcount of 50, 'all the fun gets taken out of it'. However, in the knowledge economy, many are realizing that they don't need to grow any bigger at all. Just look at Craig's List, the online classified advertising portal based in San Francisco. It has only 19 staff yet, reportedly, a turnover of over US $10 million. It exemplifies the fact that you can no longer judge the value of a business by its headcount. It also exemplifies what Harvard professor Clayton Christensen has dubbed 'disruptive technology' – the site isn't the most advanced of its kind in the world, but as a small company it is willing to do without the margins achievable by a more feature-rich technology. Instead of aiming for a smaller market of lucrative customers as a more established company might, it is offering optimal speed and simplicity to a huge market worldwide. And the formula is working.

Of course, most small or medium-sized companies in the coming decades won't have this kind of independence. Probably, they'll form part of the supply chains of a small number of transnational clients, based on highly focused service agreements. Indeed, they'll be as crucial as temporary workers to the revitalization of product and service portfolios among larger brands. Nevertheless, their sense of direction will come chiefly from the entrepreneur at the helm, even if he or she is percolating the vision of an ultimate client company. A high-performing small firm doesn't really need a business plan: the entrepreneur stipulates the parameters of what the business wants to become, but otherwise manages in a hands-off style. The hierarchy is so flat that the vision is shared as reflexively and willingly as a round of drinks after work on Friday (at least, in comparison with a medium-sized or large firm). Any long-hours culture here is based on personal excitement and commitment and a sense of personal obligation to shared goals. Corporate managers can't do this; entrepreneurial leaders can.

Of course, it's easy for such a cliquey model to become unmeritocratic, particularly when clumsy efforts are made to transplant it into a large organization. After all, if the emphasis is on loyalty and socialization, doesn't it make sense to hire your friends, or at least people of the same age and cultural background? Anyone faced with the prospect of starting their own business for the first time is likely to think first of the skill-set they can access among close acquaintances. It's human nature. Social and emotional intelligence will therefore be vital to jobseekers, particularly if they are aiming for a knowledge-based job where ideas must be generated continuously and sold emotionally to colleagues. Such qualities will also be needed by tomorrow's recruiters, if they are to balance the need for innovative teamwork with meritocratic fairness (especially where legal definitions of fairness are concerned).[3] But are Western universities producing these qualities among their graduates?

Unfortunately, only a handful of European universities are so far helping students to develop these 'soft skills'. The fraternity traditions of US colleges, by contrast, encourage them. Some progress has been made at business schools, which now increasingly offer course modules or complete MBAs focused on entrepreneurship – whether their emphasis is on writing a business plan for a start-up or on corporate venturing metrics of intrapreneurship, the underlying goal is the same: to prepare students for a world of predominantly small business units. The 'international' or 'global' MBA is also well established, aiding the shift to transnational business by exposing students to a variety of different cultures. Nevertheless, in the coming decades, large recruiters will need to find new ways to appeal to Western students long before graduation – not only to ensure they have access to the deepest possible pool of talent but also to snare any valuable intellectual property (IP) developed on their time. Most of the richest men in the world are college dropouts because they couldn't wait to get into business – today it's so easy to start up a business in the West that, for most talented students, it's an entirely reasonable, if not sensible, option. Yet most universities are still failing to stake their claim to inventions developed by their students, using their resources. Notable exceptions include Stanford, where the Office of Technology Licensing recently earned a windfall of several hundred million dollars following the successful flotation of the search engine Google (the university owns the patent for 'PageRank', Google's core technology, which was developed at the university's computer science laboratories by former students Larry Page and Sergey Brin). Yet even here the yearly income from technology licences is only just over US $40 million.

Meanwhile, the smartest companies are collaborating with specific university departments to provide students with industrial experience in return for project-work that has a rapid effect on the bottom line. The French defence group Thales has an 'Internet Technology Centre' (ITC) in Reading in the UK, which sponsors numerous PhD students and is run by a visiting professor at the University of Surrey. By involving itself with various universities on various projects, the ITC enjoys not only the benefits mentioned above but also a continuous peer-review process that enables it to shed ideas with no future before they absorb significant development funds. Initiatives like this will become increasingly vital to European clusters such as the high-tech 'Silicon Fen' around Cambridge, and in deprived areas they will be the necessary hubs for economic regeneration. At last policy makers are looking across the Atlantic in search of best practice that can be adopted in regions ranging from Northern Scandinavia to Central and Southern Europe.

Where to find the West's emerging talent

Our skills are diminishing, our education systems are lagging, our populations are ageing, so how will knowledge-based companies in the West possibly find enough talented workers to compete with Indian and Chinese rivals?

Part of the solution will be to make better use of pools of talent that have previously been underutilized. The most obvious point of focus for such efforts is the unemployed or 'economically inactive'. In the UK alone, eight million people regard themselves as unable to work, as the result of either disability or a combination of enforced early retirement and obsolescent skills. Other countries in Europe have lower but, even so, substantial high rates. This is compounded by a pattern of early retirement in Europe.

There are several social groups in the West whose skills are woefully underutilized. They're easy to find because they're the same groups presently showing the strongest growth in entrepreneurship. First and foremost, the young. We've already mentioned how today's students are becoming less and less scared of starting up their own businesses before graduation. And an increasing number are doing so even earlier – just look at Alex Tew, the 21-year-old entrepreneur behind MillionDollarHomepage.com;

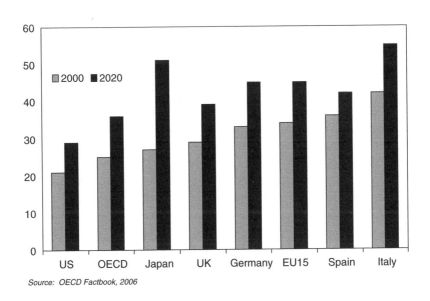

Source: OECD Factbook, 2006

Figure 3.1 Ratio of population aged 65+ to the total labour force

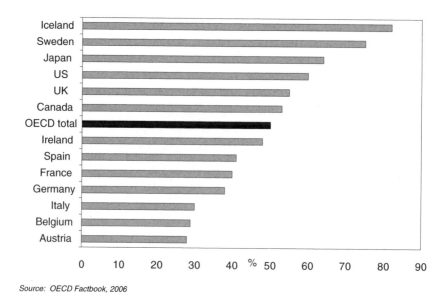

Source: OECD Factbook, 2006

Figure 3.2   Employment rates for age group 55–65 (% in employment)

before he hit the jackpot with his PR-driven internet gimmick, he
had previously started and then folded two other online businesses. A recent survey by London Business School on behalf of
the Global Entrepreneurship Monitor found that, in the UK, 69.7
per cent of 18- to 24-year-olds felt entrepreneurship was 'a good
career move'.

One of the major legacies of the dotcom boom (in spite of the
subsequent bust) was that it made young people more confident
about what could be achieved at an early age. In particular, it
made them realize that their generation – the first to be raised
on silicon – would be the most empowered by modern technology. It also demolished for good the idea that entrepreneurship
and business management were the exclusive preserve of older
men. European school systems would therefore do well to learn
from the United States, which seems to have a peerless ability to
imbue its youth with an entrepreneurial mentality. It's undoubtedly one of the factors behind America's comparative surge in
productivity in recent years. Duplicating US teaching methods
– in terms of both technical content and business values – should

be a high priority in the efforts to counterbalance Asia's entrepreneurial rise.

At the opposite end of the generational spectrum, the elderly
and 'retired' represent a huge reserve of talent that has ceased to
be tapped, largely for superficial reasons. Ageism in large corporations is still rife, particularly in Europe where equal opportunities legislation is still not adequately enforced. In many places, the
discrimination is unwitting, but everywhere it's real: people tend
to hire duplicates of themselves unless they're specifically ordered
not to. And as corporate structures become more and more
geared towards colleague sociability, the danger of unmeritocratic
hiring practices increases. Young teams want young recruits.
Indeed, youth is still considered a prerequisite for certain positions, especially those with hectic work patterns, while anyone
seeking a junior position later in life, whether as the result of a
career change or a redundancy, is still considered abnormal. After
a merger or cost-reduction campaign, older employees are often
the first to lose their jobs, partly as a result of bureaucratic con-
siderations (a higher age used to mean a higher salary bracket,
although this is increasingly not the case) and partly because of a
supposition that 'new blood' will be required.

Organizations are no longer structured on the basis that every
member of staff will work until they are 60 or 65 – but they seem
stuck with the view that someone's value diminishes to zero if
they refuse to conform to corporate norms past a certain age.
This is one of the reasons why self- and part-time employment is
an increasing attraction to men and women who have devoted
the majority of their working lives to large corporations. Any
company that continues to be so blinkered is likely to see its competitive advantage seriously damaged in the near future, not
least because the growing proportion of elderly people in
Western countries will have huge spending power, and could be
best served by people of their own age.[4] Equally, retirees have
the benefit of experience over their young rivals, making them a
valuable addition to any temporary workforce. Managed correctly, with sufficient social skills among managers to deal with
any generation gap, the over-50s can be a valuable component of
organizational flexibility. Recruiters in Europe should expect the

statutory age of retirement to be banned in the near future – as it is in the United States – for the sake of both companies that need more freedom to retain talent and individuals who wish to exploit their growing life expectancy. Certainly, they should shift their assessment of each employee's value to the results they achieve rather than any prejudiced notion of their deficiencies.

Another form of discrimination holding back the competitiveness of the West is discrimination against ethnic minorities, who are still underrepresented in senior management positions. This is in spite of the fact that both the United States and Europe have thriving economic sectors dominated by ethnic entrepreneurs. To recap: hiring from a mixture of cultures will not only be preferable but essential to your competitive advantage in the coming decades. It's how you'll generate a portfolio of products and services that genuinely reflect the cultural profile of your domestic markets, and what will give you the 'insider knowledge' to approach foreign customers with more confidence. If you have a large company and wish to survive for decades rather than just a few years then you need executives who, at the least, speak Mandarin and Hindi.

Of course, companies in the West will only benefit from immigration if they are supported by pragmatic public attitudes. That is to say, the popular culture must be more welcoming and tolerant; the media must take a more responsible role in fostering cross-cultural relations; and governments must continue to support equal opportunities for legal immigrants while clamping down on economic migrancy. According to some United Nations estimates, there are 200 million economic migrants in the world. Still, companies have a responsibility now to invest more in language training and, more generally, to foster values of tolerant citizenship. They must also recognize that, even in a situation of optimal cultural harmony, a massive immigrant population would be required to plug the skills gap in most Western countries. The UK, for example, will need an extra 200,000 immigrants a year by 2010 to maintain its economic output if it can tap no other sources of talent. Where would the US economy be without its approximately 12 million 'illegal' immigrants? Fortunately, there is another, even bigger source of talent that still hasn't been fully utilized: women.

Why business is now a women's world

Women are already vital to the economies of the West, and will become even more so as the huge populations of India and China force every other country to reject the last vestiges of sexism in favour of objective, results-focused recruitment. Forty years ago, most women were confined largely to part-time jobs. But since the feminist revolution of the 1960s and 1970s, their pursuit of qualifications and careers has been voracious. Indeed, the rise of women has in part contributed to the ageing problem now faced by the West – as their independence has increased, so the birth rate has declined. This is less significant in the United States where the fertility rate remains higher. There has been a slight increase in fertility rates in some European countries in the past five years, largely accounted for by a higher birth rate among their incoming migrant populations.

Corporate structures are still geared largely towards men – an historical legacy that dates back to the Industrial Revolution,

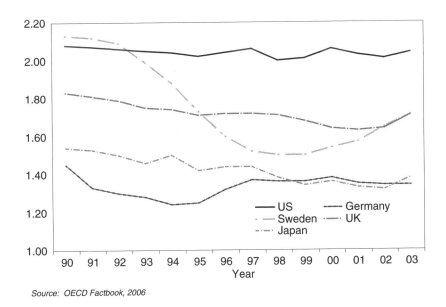

Source: OECD Factbook, 2006

Figure 3.3 Average number of children born to women aged 15–49

even though the 19th century saw the creation of all sorts of labour-saving technology. The factory was an exclusively male domain until the 20th century. Women were excluded except during times of national warfare, confined to low-paid clerical jobs, or concentrated in specific sectors such as light industry, distribution, health, welfare and education. Throughout, their primary role was unquestionably that of home-maker. Even after skill shortages brought large numbers of Western women into the workplace, tacit discrimination remained in place as the result of modern management techniques. 'Organization Man' was born, the pinstriped corporate cog who could expect to be rewarded for his loyalty and commitment with promotion and orderly career progression, and to be supported in this by his wife – emotionally, socially and administratively – while her career was either non-existent or put on the back-burner.

And so it goes on. Today, women are still passed over for promotion for spurious reasons – often because they are judged to lack the assertive qualities needed to lead projects or departments, even though they are highly technically competent. Too many men are promoting in their own image, often under the illusion that women still bow to the primacy of their partners' careers, and will therefore abandon their own positions at the drop of a hat. Today in the UK, women account for only 5 per cent of top managers and only 30 per cent of middle-managers. The rest are concentrated in jobs that are low-paid and part-time; support-oriented (again, tacitly subservient to male superiors in secretarial, customer service or administrative roles); excluded from core business management processes (but located in, for example, human resources, which most corporations have yet to recognize as a department of vital strategic importance); and excluded from male-dominated networks to the point where they gather in women-friendly sectors such as health and welfare, retail, hospitality and the media.

The outcome of all this exclusion has been a surge in women's entrepreneurship in the United States and Europe – significantly, often with a lower incidence of business failure than that experienced by men in similar economic sectors. This pattern is confirmed by data collected by London Business School's Global

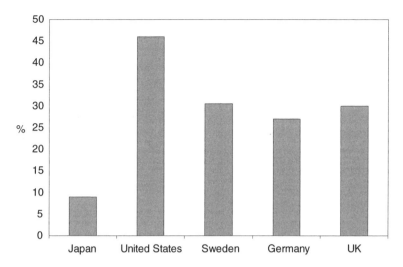

Source: After H. Deresky, *International Management: Managing Across Borders and Cultures*, 1st ed. 2006, Prentice Hall

Figure 3.4   Percentage of managers who are women

Entrepreneurship Monitor. It is also confirmed by research undertaken by Babson College that shows women-led businesses in Massachusetts are strong engines of economic growth. Forty-two per cent of these businesses grew by more than 5 per cent (2002–3), far greater than the national economic expansion rate.

It has also led to a harmful lack of diversity in the culture of management, with too many companies now viewing their markets through the blinkers of old, white, middle-aged men.

Recruiting women in greater numbers and making provision for their specific needs should be a no-brainer for any forward-looking business in the West. Notwithstanding the fact that diversity fuels innovation, companies in the knowledge economy need managers who are more empathetic, mutually supportive, team-oriented and willing to share. These are qualities that women have in abundance owing to the peer-group socialization they've practised since childhood. In ideas-based organizations there *should* be no room for individual competition, hoarding of information, one-upmanship or any other feature of so-called 'macho' management cultures.

What's more, women make over 90 per cent of all consumer purchasing decisions. It's a figure you can't afford to ignore if you're in the business of selling any kind of consumer-oriented product or service – if you're planning to hire managers from India and China with a view to getting closer to your customers, then why not make them women? After all, your foremost loyalty should be to the global constituency that already accounts for most of your sales.

Of course, women will still face gender-specific challenges as they rise through the corporate ranks. It has always been difficult for women to juggle senior positions with their domestic roles and, in the fluid, knowledge-based company of tomorrow, maternity and paternity leave could have more serious consequences than ever before. At the same time male roles will have to be redefined. When the emphasis is on short-term projects and performance-related rewards, the loss of a key member of staff at a critical time could have the same effect it would have in a small company. What's more, as jobs will be less clearly defined than they were in the past, so it will become more difficult to replace specialized or senior individuals for any significant length of time, unless they have made provision for some kind of 'organizational memory' of their precise role. In traditional bureaucracies, jobs are defined explicitly, making employees more dispensable and substitutable. In the future, any individual with unique and mission-critical knowledge will have greater security but will also have to show much greater commitment if the wider organization is not to suffer.

Equally, companies must prepare for a job market in which women will shop around for job definitions, perks and corporate structures that allow them to fulfil their personal ambitions without turning into men at the office. In particular, they must appeal to women with children by providing options for flexible and remote working; and childcare facilities such as on-site crèches. Government support will be crucial too, in matters such as maternity and paternity leave. Indeed, the same legislation that businesses have complained about vociferously in recent years will actually become crucial to Western competitiveness.

The first evidence of this trend can already be seen in Stockholm, Sweden, and Helsinki, Finland, which are presently among the top cities in the world for entrepreneurial growth. This is despite the strict imposition of family-friendly laws and maternity and paternity leave as well as working hours directives. These Scandinavian countries also have the highest percentages of women in top political and public-sector occupations.

Turning companies into talent farms

Why do chief executives complain about skills shortages every time there's an economic upturn? The cynical answer is that it suits them to draw attention from their own failures to recruit and train staff by slamming those in the local public education system. A more generous inference would be that the average company still doesn't recognize the importance of its role as an educator. Most still fail to allocate enough resources to training and they often practise false economies such as preventing staff from educating themselves on company time. Meanwhile, most knowledge-workers are expected to 'learn on the job', picking up the skills they need through informal dialogue with colleagues. It's a situation that's especially common when someone has been promoted internally, and then is expected to take on a new role without sufficient time, tuition or shadowing to develop the new skills required. As workers switch jobs, companies and even careers more frequently over the coming decades, HR departments will have to ensure that their training regimes are as flexible as the organizational structures around them. MBA programmes and executive education have expanded in recent years but, in non-management ranks, the value of on-the-job training is still being neglected, while job descriptions in too many organizations still seem to be cast in stone.

This rigidity and lack of foresight are a legacy of the scientific management style of most of the 20th century, when jobs were based on strict, immutable criteria and there was believed to be only one 'right' way of doing things. Back then, work-study engineers, management consultants and cost accountants tried to assess and define managerial tasks in quantifiable terms. They outlined 'best practice' in a variety of strategic and operational areas and, while developing many valuable principles that remain valid, failed to add the disclaimer that the biggest successes always result from non-conformist thinking. Ultimately, their attitudes drove the expansion of higher education in both the United States and Europe, with its emphasis on formal qualifications (both academic and vocational). It became the duty of higher education institutions to produce graduates who could be slotted directly into corporate hierarchies. In turn, this reinforced the caste-like character of major companies.

Meanwhile, the many personal talents that can't be assessed through formal qualifications have been grossly underutilized. The 'soft skills' that will improve team-working and customer relations, and that will generate the most innovative products and services through customer empathy, are in many organizations still confined to the low-paid ranks of supposedly unskilled individuals, with no system in place to detect and nurture them. In some organizations, a couple of mediocre grades on your CV can render you permanently 'unsuitable for promotion'. The qualifications meant to encourage meritocracy are in fact undermining it.

To overcome these problems, it's not enough for a company simply to make a commitment to the continuous improvement of staff skills and knowledge – there are already many organizations, especially in the public sector, where this attitude simply reinforces the way things have been done in the past. Instead, you must look for potential and then realize it. A useful model to emulate is that of successful football teams, where managers know that success is not guaranteed simply by paying huge sums for the best talent. A star footballer may be purchased on the basis of a track record that shows potential, but this potential can only be realized after intensive on-the-job training with other players in the team. Crucially, the player must learn to cooperate with his or her new team-members to understand their tactics and develop empathy and shared understanding.

High-performing companies also judge the value of experience by looking at its breadth as well as its depth, since the increasingly project-based and decentralized nature of the modern corporation needs workers with an holistic skill-set, who can multi-task and move sideways across the company in order to exploit its fluid, responsive structure.

Of course, the most valuable skill in the knowledge economy is the one you can't teach. Creativity can be nurtured and leveraged through tolerance of non-conformity and dissent, but is notoriously difficult to detect in potential recruits. Yes, you can learn a lot about an interviewee by asking them to come up with ideas on the fly. But the best innovations are generally context-specific – that is, they occur at a confluence of incongruous circumstances. And while creative people are rare, those who quickly and reliably grasp the value of their ideas are even rarer.

What we can say for sure is that value-driven creativity tends to be greatest in people who possess three distinct types of intelligence. First, intellectual intelligence, which is traditionally graded by academic qualifications but more usefully assessed through conceptualization exercises. Any company wishing to improve its rate of innovation needs people who can think in abstract terms like a research scientist, a mathematician or a writer. Second, emotional intelligence, which manifests itself in qualities such as self-confidence, intuition and empathy. And third, social intelligence (also known as charisma): the ability to communicate, cooperate and motivate, to promote ideas and arguments compellingly and coherently. It's the second and third of these qualities that will soon be essential to any company wishing to leverage the insights of the first in the form of innovative products and services. Unfortunately, these obtain the least attention, from educators through to corporate HR departments.

Earning staff commitment in a disloyal world

Around 80 per cent of workers in the West today say they feel little or no commitment to their employers, yet many major companies still believe that commitment is something to be bought rather than earned.

It's an attitude that has its roots in the bureaucratic companies of the 20th century, where personal achievement was clearly graded in terms of age-related prestige, pay and fringe benefits. Here, ranks and status symbols acted as a transparent benchmarking system, with powerful tacit meanings attached to certain offices, parking spaces or the awe-inspiring 'keys to the executive washroom'. Ultimately, a brighter future was guaranteed to those who climbed the stepladder of the company hierarchy, making it much easier to bear any necessary sacrifices along the way. Workers would devote the whole of their working lives to one company on the basis that wages would increase with age and employment was guaranteed until the legal age of retirement.

Today, 'jobs for life' no longer exist, and so-called full-time positions in the knowledge economy are insecure. Mergers and acquisitions can leave people adrift in their 30s if they're made redundant, as market 'shake-outs' produce regional skills gluts. There's no longer such an obvious stepladder for promotion: people with the talent to reach the top tend to move sideways repeatedly. And youth confidence in the post-dotcom era is breaking the connection between age ranges and specific positions. More fundamentally, the project-based, intrapreneurial structure that will be prevalent among larger companies in the coming decades is inherently short-termist. A high-performing company is necessarily a restless place, so it must be careful not to breed restless employees who make only token gestures of commitment, while keeping one eye on the door.

For now, the prevailing method of generating employee commitment in the West is still instrumental – that is to say, it motivates using performance-related reward systems. This may have been adequate in the past, at companies where jobs and their outputs were clearly defined (often in negotiation with trade unions), with standard rates for specific jobs, designed to reflect skills, training and responsibilities. However, most employees now perform tasks that cannot easily be measured in relation to explicit criteria of output and performance. In today's service-based companies, remuneration levels are increasingly at the discretion of business unit managers, making the instrumental reward system less transparent and less meaningful.

The instrumental system also breeds workers who are unwilling to question or challenge the status quo. After all, who wants to stick their head above the parapet and question operational practices or product and service portfolios when there could be another wave of redundancies around the corner? The best way to demonstrate commitment here is through personal visibility, a major factor in the long-working-hours cultures of the United States and the UK. Low rates of organizational change and innovation are the inevitable results of such a malaise. Structures intended to aid creativity can actually have the inverse effect if paycheques and perks are the only ways to ensure employee attendance.

Many companies believe mistakenly that by offering high material rewards and by deliberately encouraging an instrumental attitude amongst their employees they will enhance performance. But if so, it's usually only in the short term. The result is a 'buccaneer' culture when everyone, including the managers, works for their own ends and plays the system. What typically happens is that the culture becomes excessively competitive, with jealous feuding over share options, bonuses and salaries. Perhaps the best-known example of this behaviour was at the collapsed US energy firm Enron, which used a so-called 'rank and yank' system to periodically threaten the lowest-performing 15 per cent of its workforce with the sack.[5] Overarching corporate values are forgotten when fiefdoms develop and wage inequality increases.

The prevalence of all this internal corporate competitiveness means that the average modern worker lives for today, judging their own success in terms of material rewards they can reap now rather build towards in the future. In part, this is a product of higher youth expectations in the West, but it's also the product of job insecurity – a sense that you have to grab what you can while you can. And it's connected to our modern consumer culture in which shopping around is expected. Why stay working for a company you hate when you spend most of your life there? For young professionals in the West, who are guaranteed a pretty good standard of living no matter what they do, a career is just another lifestyle choice.

These trends are reflected in high rates of churn in the West, where the average occupancy of the CEO's position is now around three or four years. In the knowledge economy, it's easier for people to walk away from their jobs and set up somewhere else, because they're not tied to machinery bolted to the floor as in the old factories. Meanwhile, among junior workers 'resentful compliance' (holding a job reluctantly because you have no better option) is still widespread. It's a low-trust environment in which managers think they know best and junior workers do as little as they can get away with, exemplified by the automobile industries of Europe in the 1960s and the large sectors of shop-floor employees in the traditional manufacturing companies of the 20th century.

Trade unionism was both a cause and effect of resentful compliance in that it forced management to negotiate and fix the parameters of certain jobs, regardless of market conditions, technological developments or flexible business practices. The result was completely unadaptable internal corporate structures in certain sectors, coupled with frequent industrial disputes. Other effects included high levels of absenteeism and staff turnover.

France, Germany and the southern European countries still have bureaucratic structures in many of their public- and private-sector organizations, but in the United States and the UK there's a big shift under way, driven largely by advances in information technology (IT) that allow processes to be monitored by machines rather than managers. In the coming decades, traditional forms of motivation will be less capable of generating commitment among employees, and will ultimately be a hindrance to the competitive advantage of most organizations.

Appealing to hearts and minds, as well as wallets

Attractive material rewards are necessary to recruit and (superficially at least) to retain the best talent. But to optimize their performance, companies need to ensure that the commitment of their employees is psychologically internalized. That is to say, they must create conditions in which staff actively want to get in early and stay late, and are willing to put huge effort into their jobs because they associate the company's success with their own. What's required is an employment relationship (rather than simply a wage contract), under which the employee regards him or herself as a stakeholder in the long-term success of the company.

So how do you create these conditions? The two-day, off-site culture-building activity is likely to bear some fruit. But in addition you need to invest in training programmes and facilities that enable staff to develop personally, as well as professionally. You need to overturn the traditional view of 'working to live', under which your staff work merely to generate the resources of time and money to pursue things they actually enjoy. Give them reasonable time and space to enjoy those things during supposed working hours and you will create a powerful disincentive to resignation. At present, most of us suffer the worst of all worlds from our employers. We are given performance targets and then 'watched' by our bosses as we struggle to achieve them. It forces us to carry on commuting into the same congested stations at the same time every day despite the opportunities for home and remote working offered by the capabilities of broadband technologies.

To be a high-performing company, you need to give your staff as much freedom and personal autonomy as possible within the parameters of an overarching corporate vision and values. In other words, you need to let workers achieve the tasks you set them in their own time and on their own terms, with a more amenable blend of life and work. A very high proportion of the tasks of most knowledge-workers can be completed at home, and in the coming decades competitiveness will depend on shifting an increasing number out of the office. Notwithstanding the increased number of women entering the workforce, companies will have to make greater provision for flexible hours, remote working and childcare provision. Indeed, the most progressive will be helping their employees remove onerous tasks from both their personal and professional lives, by providing everything from financial advice to personal fitness training at the work-place. You also need to nullify the operational frustrations that act as a bar to commitment by making it clear that you not only tolerate but actively encourage constructive dissent.

Unfortunately, this latter effort isn't helped by the myth-making now surrounding many corporate celebrities, who win their positions with huge fanfare and spin, as if they can turn around any business single-handedly. PR officers will typically claim that the dizzying remuneration package of a new CEO reflects global market forces and performance-related systems as well as the intrinsic demands of the job, yet they rarely spell out the detailed criteria on which the sums are based. Certainly, a CEO's role is never spelt out with the same precision as that of a shop-floor worker in a 20th-century manufacturer. It's an attempt to apply an instrumental model to a nebulous job description, and frequently it spells disaster: just look at the fate of recent chief executives at Coca-Cola, Disney, Hewlett-Packard and many other companies. In the near future, investors are going to reject this inflation of the value of corporate celebrities in favour of a return to long-term leadership: the ultimate answer to the instrumental reward system.

Today's employees in the West are a cynical generation. They haven't been handed a work ethic by their parents because, in all likelihood, one or both of their parents have been scarred by their employment experiences. Why make a commitment to any company if your dad was rewarded for 27 years of service with redundancy or early retirement brought on by corporate mergers and acquisitions and by an ageist system? In turn, many parents see instilling the work ethic as the responsibility of teachers and the education system. But, ultimately, it is the responsibility of companies, and what many now need – especially those based in the West – are fewer managers and more leaders.

Endnotes

1 The instant production line: In 2000, Microsoft decided it wanted a slice of the burgeoning digital home entertainment market. Its problem was that, as a software producer, it knew very little about how to manufacture, say, a games console to rival the Sony PlayStation. And

it certainly didn't have the facilities. Enter Flextronics, a contract-manufacturer based in Singapore, with offices and assembly lines in over 30 countries. It collaborated with chip manufacturer Intel, and used its own components manufactured in-house, to make the hardware as cost-effective as possible within Microsoft's parameters on function and performance. Today, Flextronics can churn out several hundred thousand Xboxes in a month, depending on demand. Its turnover in 2005 was around US $15.9 billion.

2 'Knowledge Transfer through Inheritance: Spin-out Generation, Development and Performance', *Academy of Management Journal*, 2004, by Dr Rajshree Agarwal, associate professor of strategic management at the University of Illinois at Urbana-Champaign, with Raj Echambadi, April Franco and MB Sarkar.

3 Selective sandwich-makers: At Pret A Manger, the UK-based chain of sandwich and coffee shops, the junior staff hire each other. Anyone applying to join the chain as a shop assistant goes through a standard vetting procedure involving CVs and interviews. Then, if they make it to the short-list, they join the team in a real outlet for a day. At 4 pm, the rest of the team-members are asked to vote 'yes' or 'no' on a napkin to the idea of the newcomer becoming a permanent fixture. The process helps to avoid personality clashes before they develop, and enhances the social networks at a local level.

4 Old but not out of date: B&Q, the international chain of home improvement stores, employs 6,300 people aged over 50 at its 320 UK stores – about 19 per cent of the total workforce. In 1991, it opened a store in Macclesfield staffed entirely by people over the age of 50. Two years later, independent research showed that the store performed equally well as or better than an average B&Q store in terms of sales, profit, staff turnover and customer satisfaction. Experience, knowledge and attitude were judged to be the attributes most beneficial to the quality of customer service.

5 Rank, yank and regret: Can you identify the best 20 per cent of your workforce, and the worst 20 per cent? Many companies do so on a regular basis in order to stimulate underperformers with the threat of redundancy. It's a system that was advocated and used to ruthless effect at General Electric under its former CEO Jack Welch. He maintains that it's a humane way to let people know how they're doing so that redundancy, if it happens, doesn't come as a shock to

them. But at Enron, the system was widely regarded as a major factor in the company's failure. The essential problem with 'rank and yank' is that, once all the weak employees are expelled, further sackings don't necessarily improve performance. Instead, they lead to cutthroat politics and low morale that ultimately damage productivity and encourage cheating. At Enron, managers became so desperate to maintain performance that they created hundreds of off-the-book 'entities' to hide or disguise heavy debts and losses. By the end, the company had become so paranoid that it had recruited numerous former CIA and FBI agents to enforce security.

4 Cut the managers and bring in the leaders

Farewell to managers and hello to leaders

- Managers are the bureaucratic organization
- Why we still need bureaucracy
- Leadership – admiration, inspiration and trust
- Loosen up creativity and innovation
- You can't tell people what to do any more
- MBAs as corporate lieutenants – not celebrities

Say the word 'managers' to any young person in the West and they'll probably imagine people formally dressed, refusing to accept that there are better ways of doing things and refusing to socialize with anyone they consider beneath themselves. In other words, managers are seen to be the antithesis of creativity, the quality most needed by the majority of Western companies if they are to compete with fast-emerging rivals in India, China and even Brazil and the emerging market economies of Poland, the Czech Republic and other EU states.

Managers are people who control but don't necessarily enable. In the 19th century, they disseminated orders on behalf of company bosses and supervised groups of workers on their behalf. Then, at the turn of the 20th century, their job descriptions were extended to include the pursuit of efficiency. Under the fashionable 'scientific management' theory of Frederick Wilmslow Taylor, a US engineer, they were encouraged to identify the most productive workers, examine the ways they worked and then instruct everyone else to follow suit. Under the theory, productivity was also boosted by matching people to their ideal jobs based on physical attributes. When Taylor became a manager at Bethlehem Steel, Pennsylvania, in 1898, he noticed that every worker was given the same-sized shovel, regardless of their strength. Simply by issuing bigger shovels to bigger workers, he was able to slash the company's costs, and its workforce, in half. Over the following decades, his ideas were adopted by companies all over the world and a gap opened up between the managers who devised operational processes and the workers who executed them. Management became a discipline in its own right, and its practitioners began to equate themselves with commissioned military officers, superior in intellect, education and even breeding to the lesser-skilled ranks under their command.

Amazingly, this division still exists today – it's why the hypothetical managers described above are so recognizable. In the West, the majority of organizations have a management structure that is only good at sending information in one direction: from the top to the bottom. Only a minority have realized the value of drawing information up the chain of command, despite the fact that front-line and operational workers tend to have the most contact with products, services and customers. Even fewer have processes in place to spread valuable information from side to side, so that managers and workers at every level can make sure they aren't duplicating one another's efforts or struggling unnecessarily with a problem that has been solved by a colleague on the next floor. In most organizations, to challenge the accepted way of doing things is to challenge the authority of your boss. That makes you a troublemaker.

Many of Taylor's ideas remain valid. He's unfairly criticized for being the father of corporate rigidity when in fact he was among the first to argue in favour of the continuous technical development of workers and incentive-based pay structures. But in the coming decades his methods will be confined increasingly to industries in which the majority of workers perform repetitive tasks, such as fast-food, call-centre operations and certain types of manufacturing that have yet to be automated. They may also be applicable to more lucrative services, as the advance of information and communications technology makes it easier to commoditize the processing of information, and to monitor the performance of remote knowledge-workers.

In short, Taylorism will enable companies in India and China to continue undercutting Western rivals. Meanwhile, in the United States and Europe, perversely it will actually erode competitive advantage wherever it remains the prevailing management culture. In a knowledge-based, professional service business, the more managers you have, the more constrained you are. If you force your employees to traverse two or three layers of management for permission to put their ideas into practice then you will see a decline in morale, trust and commitment. If, on the other hand, you ensure that the ideas of every employee are acknowledged, acted upon and rewarded then you will incentivize the creation of new business opportunities and efficiencies. The less you treat an individual like a small cog in a large machine, the more creative potential you'll unlock.

Thankfully, corporate hierarchies have been flattening in parallel with the decline of Western manufacturing, but if companies in the United States and Europe are to withstand the coming surge in Asian services then they must act now to make better use of their human resources. The time has come for managers to shift their focus from controlling their staff to liberating them.

Tomorrow's leaders: more than just managers in tights and capes

Managers get their authority from whichever corporate rank is displayed on their business card, the door of their office or the

Toblerone-shaped stick on their desk. Leaders get their authority from personal qualities such as self-confidence, empathy and, in spite of its vague definition, charisma. Even in the armed forces, ranking officers will fail to get the best out of those they command unless their own courage, skill and sense of sacrifice are beyond dispute.

You can't be a leader by proxy, threatening to take your concerns about someone up the chain of command when they underperform. All this attitude will produce is instrumental compliance, a superficial commitment based on financial expediency. Anyone who has seen the popular US and UK sitcom *The Office* may regard the ineffectual character of this business unit manager as the worst kind of middle-manager, but in many ways he has the right ideas – socializing with staff, encouraging a casual and open dialogue between ranks. He just does these things badly, and in wilful ignorance of his company's overall performance and objectives. What he lacks and what Western managers need are qualities born of social experience and professional excellence.

Look at the business section of any bookshop and you'll find dozens of titles about the art (or science) of leadership, each claiming to provide the secret managerial recipe guaranteed to win hearts and minds. Boiled down, the essential ingredients are as follows.

First, *admiration*. If your staff don't admire you, they won't feel the need to impress you. The source of their admiration can be grounded in your technical expertise, the results you have achieved for the company, your ability to resolve disputes or build teams – anything, so long as it's visible, unassailable and sufficiently unique among your peers. Jack Welch suggests that 'respect' is an innate quality that arises intuitively and can't be learnt; the management theorist Tom Peters suggests that it is a by-product of successful 'self-branding'. Ultimately, it is dependent on a good reputation, the attribute that enables corporate celebrities to move from company to company and still be admired by whichever workforce they happen to command.

Second, *inspiration*. Remember how it feels to be truly inspired by someone? Probably, we admired them enough to listen in the first place or, if not, we admired them soon after. Either way, we still needed to be intrigued, persuaded and enthused by their ideas. Being inspirational obviously depends on developing good communication skills. Equally, it depends on choosing the right ideas in the first place and selling them in the right way by fully understanding your audience. It marries a full understanding of the company's future threats and opportunities with an empathy for those who need to be persuaded of your strategies. Finally, it depends on finding ways to be non-conformist and, therefore, exciting. After all, if leadership depended on consensus then it wouldn't be leadership at all.

Third, *trust*. Tomorrow's leaders have to be trusted completely by those under their command, and in turn they have to trust their staff to take on an increasing number of responsibilities. In a knowledge-based company, where reporting structures, teams and job descriptions change continually, trust is the grout between the tiles. It represents a social, psychological contract that reduces the need for bureaucratic checks and balances and thereby reduces the constraints on creativity, constructive dissent and personal initiative. It's an essential feature for any workplace that wishes to boost its performance while becoming more informal, sociable and tolerant of personal preferences in the way working practices are organized.

A leader builds trust by taking a facilitative, enabling approach to management, nurturing the skills, capabilities and enthusiasm of their staff. Along the way, they'll need to make full use of interpersonal skills that were never required of the traditional managers who deliberately distanced themselves from staff using a secretary or a closed office door. To reiterate, women have a natural advantage here: thanks to their ability to form emotional bonds, they'll become increasingly vital to the leadership of Western companies.

'You must be the change you wish to see in the world'

Mahatma Gandhi was right: the best way to lead people is to embody the things you believe in. Half a century after his death, we all have a fairly clear image of this man in our heads, partly because his achievements left him pictured in a thousand school textbooks and partly because Sir Ben Kingsley depicted him so convincingly on film in 1982, but primarily because, to Western eyes, he looked and behaved so oddly. Gandhi wove his own clothes – a traditional Indian dhoti and shawl – because he wanted to be able to appeal to the poorest people in India. In business terms, he embodied his own 'mission': one of humility, self-sufficiency and pacifism while at the same time having a potent 'vision' of India without British rule.

The words 'mission' and 'vision', as they apply to corporate statements of principle and purpose, have become confused and even interchangeable in recent years. They're regarded with cynicism by many workers in the West, because of their tendency to change at the urging of management consultants, and because – like any jargon – they are a reminder of management at its worst: aloof, obfuscating and detached from reality. Nevertheless, they can be very useful if they are properly defined, and both are essential to leadership, no matter what titles they are given.

In its original and most useful sense, a mission statement is a definition of the goals that give an enterprise its identity. So, for example, Wal-Mart's reads: 'To give ordinary folk the chance to buy the same thing as rich people.' (A nicely spun reminder of the social benefits of shaving every possible cent from the wholesale costs of your suppliers.) Similarly, Disney gives itself the following mantra: 'We create happiness by providing the finest in entertainment to people of all ages, everywhere.' These are public statements that everyone can buy into: customers, stakeholders and staff. By contrast, a vision statement was originally intended to be a snapshot of the future, an internal benchmarking target involving, say, financial results or market share. (If in doubt, remember that a vision statement adheres to the acronym SMART – specific, measurable, achievable, realistic, time-bound.)

Unfortunately, many companies in the West have, in recent years, adopted statements of both types that are too ambitious, vague, nebulous, complex or derivative. Mission statements often run to 100 words or more, with some acting as a wish-list rather than an accurate reflection of what distinguishes the company from its rivals. Vision statements often espouse vague ideals of quality, or set unrealistic, morale-sapping targets. Elsewhere, they are amalgamated to produce glib lists of bullet points that no one ever reads. Most importantly, the vast majority of Western companies fail to invest them with any kind of unique selling point. That is to say, they give their company an identity without making sure it is unique. The rise of India and China makes such oversights unacceptable. Soon, only a clearly articulated sense of principle, purpose and *differentiation* will enable professional service companies in the West to justify the value-added premiums they charge over their Asian rivals.

Both mission and vision have to be specific enough to distinguish the company from others and general enough to allow for the kind of personal interpretation and initiative required in the trust-based corporate structures of tomorrow. Moreover, to generate competitive advantage they have to be accepted willingly, as ideals rather than as diktats from above. This is where leadership rather than management becomes vital, especially in a business that produces no physical products. Knowledge doesn't have a sensory quality, making it difficult for knowledge-workers to gauge the difference they are making and feel motivated as a result.

A good leader overcomes such problems by being a good storyteller. That is to say, he or she is able to demonstrate to an individual worker how their role contributes to the overall goals of the company. As Tom Peters puts it: 'Don't create a business, create a cause.' Perhaps the most famous demonstration of this principle concerns the apocryphal janitor at Cape Canaveral in Florida who, when asked to describe his job, said: 'I'm helping to put a man on the moon.' Admittedly, such views are easier to find when the mission is patriotic – indeed, any public-sector organization should appeal continually to its employees' sense of civic duty if it doesn't do so already. Nevertheless, a mission statement based on, say, a quality-of-life premise can be effective too. For example, the airline Virgin Atlantic says it wants: 'To grow a profitable airline that people love to fly and where people love to work.' Note how this is designed to make staff feel as valued as customers, while reminding them that only sustained profitability can make the 'love' a reality. It doesn't offer much differentiation from other airlines, but that doesn't matter too much when the boss, Richard Branson, publicly embodies the excitement and left-field thinking he offers to his staff, and expects from them in return. In this sense, his death-defying adventures in hot air balloons are comparable to Gandhi's public displays of asceticism.

Of course, leadership in business can never be purely symbolic – it will always involve traditional management tasks. The essential challenges for Western leaders as they attempt to extract more value from their workers will be to balance issues such as quality control, regulatory compliance and robust financial reporting with increasing levels of personal freedom and informality. In other words, they have to find ways to make work less boring without the company falling into disarray. Happily, this process can be a virtuous circle. Some jobs can be enriched in parallel with customer experience – for example, many US retailers are now training security personnel to actively help visitors to their stores. Similarly, in service companies, it is worth focusing on junior knowledge-workers, who are often the most frustrated by the repetitiveness of their jobs while simultaneously being in the best position to come up with valuable innovations. Simple acts of recognition can be enough to boost their levels of innovation and commitment.

The need for pervasive leadership

We tend to think of leadership as something confined to the top of an organization. But if Western companies are going to be optimally competitive in the coming decades then they need to practise pervasive leadership. That is to say, they must ensure that their managers at every level learn and apply leadership skills. Why? Because most companies of the future will be disaggregated and project-based, and only strong leadership will keep their disparate parts travelling in the same direction.

The pyramid management structure is fading into obscurity. In fact, its usage has been diminishing for decades. In the 1980s, Western companies began to flatten their management hierarchies. In the 1990s, they embraced the ideas of business process re-engineering, breaking themselves down into customer-focused trading units – subsidiary companies or internal profit-and-loss centres. These principles were applied as vigorously to public-sector bodies such as hospitals, schools, universities, social-service departments and large sectors of national government as they were to private-sector companies.

The prevailing Western management culture is project-based, suited to organizational structures composed of many small, semi-autonomous units, each with their own operational targets, key success factors and performance-related reward system. Such an incumbent culture is proving helpful now that globalization is forcing Western companies to disaggregate internationally. However, it is also inherently short-termist, with the head of each unit focused on completion of their current project. The idea of being permitted to find your own way of working may sound liberating – for example, if you or your team are given an objective and left to determine your own hours and operational processes – but under such circumstances it is easy to underestimate how much time a task will take to complete (as any freelance will testify), and difficult to build redundancy into the schedule. As a consequence, you can be stuck working long hours, like so many other knowledge-workers in the United States and the UK.

In projects where only the success criteria and the deadline matter, the danger is that the quality of work, not to mention the worker's well-being, can suffer. After all, are you really going to allow yourself to 'clock off' at 5 pm or take your full entitlement of annual leave if a high proportion of your potential income depends on meeting a deadline that requires you to stay late? It's a situation that can be exploited by unscrupulous senior managers who wish to extract unpaid overtime from the leaders and teams beneath them, or who wish to abdicate certain responsibilities by claiming they have been delegated. Similarly, the leaders of semi-autonomous operating units can act as Little

Hitlers who, instead of bringing the best out of their staff, create hierarchical fiefdoms of their own, regarding their areas of responsibility as personal assets. Even without such behaviour, the system encourages staff to feel loyal to their immediate team rather than the company as a whole.

Any organization that wishes to become more flexible while retaining its unity of purpose must ensure that each of its managers, from the corporate celebrity downwards, has the leadership skills to bind and channel the efforts of other managers and teams under their command.

Whether this pervasive leadership can be applied internationally is another matter. The prevailing management culture in Continental Europe is still very different from that of the United States and the UK, in spite of the gradual Americanization of management best practice in recent decades. The principles of business process re-engineering have never been fully accepted in France, Germany and other major economies. There, many companies continue to use the bureaucratic models that delivered economic growth for their economies throughout the 20th century – models based on hierarchical management, clearly defined job descriptions and explicit channels of reporting. Their decision-making, although incorporating consultative processes, remains essentially top-down.

Moreover, we know that US management principles aren't necessarily applicable everywhere. The growth of Japanese companies in the 1960s and 1970s showed that there were effective alternatives. And in the 1990s, Russia's hasty moves towards free-market capitalism, in part the result of some blithe advice from US management consultancies, were a disaster. While corporate law struggled to catch up, corrupt middle-managers – many of them associated with the Mafia – were able to siphon off cash through standalone business units in which they had suddenly been given operational autonomy.

Meanwhile, in China's burgeoning private sector, companies no longer need to adhere to state planning and are thus scrambling to learn about business strategy, sending their young employees to Western business schools whence they return with the tools to give them competitive advantage on a global scale. (So many have made the journey in recent years that they have been given a nickname, 'Sea Turtles'.) Here too, the psychological contract between employers and workers is being redefined.

The country could benefit from its lack of an incumbent private-sector management culture by jumping straight into a post-Taylorist environment, in which the flexible structures described above add high levels of innovation to its low cost-base. However, the easiest way for Chinese entrepreneurs to make money in the short-to-medium term will be to continue forming partnerships with Western firms, with their mature brands and innovative impetus. Indeed, one of the reasons China has encouraged joint ventures between foreign and domestic companies in its coastal regions is to bring in Western management practices.

The challenge for China's politicians will be to manage the cultural differences that naturally result from increased penetration of Western firms into its domestic economy. Leaders of Western companies need to develop their awareness and understanding of such cultural differences in order to direct their offshore business units successfully. The discipline of management is in the process of adapting – managing cultural diversity is now a core component of most MBA and executive training programmes. But increasingly best practice will be disseminated by international supply chains, as Western companies pressure their Asian subsidiaries and partner-companies to adopt more flexible, efficient and innovation-oriented cultures; and as they adopt whichever Asian practices are necessary to align them fully with their fastest-growing markets.

How leaders create creators

As we discussed in Chapter 2, a company's structure, physical environment and reward systems are key factors in any 'culture of creativity'. Leadership is another. Bad managers have a tendency to stifle creativity because it can threaten the status quo, and because nobody ever got fired for conforming. Good leaders encourage all their workers to step forward with ideas, no matter how radical.

Many Western companies have tried in recent decades to encourage open communication between managers and their staff, using tools such as '360° feedback', which can allow low-ranking workers to sound off about their bosses. However, in most companies staff still keep ideas to themselves because they're afraid of being seen as critical and uncooperative, or because they think: 'Why should I show my line manager my best ideas if only he/she is going to benefit from them?' A good leader can nullify these attitudes by promoting the 'trust-based' culture described above, in which workers are willing to share ideas in the knowledge that they will be recognized and rewarded for doing so, rather than criticized for sticking their heads above the parapet. However, this must be coupled with a very high tolerance for mistakes. Most companies, especially those outside the United States, still regard failure as the hall-mark of an intrinsically poor performer, ignoring the fact that it can be a salutary experience. Given that the business world will soon be dominated by rapid, highly focused entrepreneur-ial or intrapreneurial projects, it's worth remembering that venture capitalists always prefer to back bosses with 'scar tissue', signs that they have learnt from failure and become stronger as a result.[1]

Anyway, in a knowledge-based company, the creative process is nearly always collaborative. Sure, you can come up with an idea on your own, but you can't prototype it in the way an individual engineer designer might. You need to sell your idea internally before you can sell it externally, which again calls for the sociable, informal and trust-based culture that only strong leadership can hold together. Many companies still take a bureaucratic approach to innovation by trying to stan-dardize the development of new products and services – say, with three months of blue-sky thinking, three months of testing and then three months of feasibility assessments. But increasingly this type of model will be too slow and cumber-some to produce a competitive advantage. The leader of a small company can now pounce on an idea that sounds promising, energize the team that created it and, thanks to modern communications technology, realize it within weeks or days. The only way for the leader of a medium-sized or large rival to achieve the same level of flexibility is by mimicking small-company structures and attitudes, and the informal style of work that goes with them.

The idea of a leader walking around his office in an open-neck shirt that hangs out of his trousers, greeting his staff as if they were equals, holding few formal meetings but agreeing to things quickly based on broad, informal consultations, and then socializing with staff outside office hours, was unthinkable before the dotcom era, and still flies in the face of organizational best practice. Yet his (or, more likely, her) company will be the one outperforming its sectoral average in the coming decades.

How to lead your company through continual change

If you're continually setting up new partnerships and joint ventures across the world, predominantly at high speed and for the short term, with a view to getting payback on your investments much faster than in the past, then you need to keep on adapting. A culture of complacency can't go unpunished any more, especially not in Western companies, which are handicapped by their high cost-base and legacy systems (in terms of organizational architecture as well as people, processes and equipment).

The average life of a company before it is sold, merged or taken over is now six or seven years. Business models have always lost their effectiveness over time but the average sell-by date is becoming shorter than ever. Consider Marks & Spencer (M&S), the UK's giant clothing and premium food retailer. Ten years ago, it was a case study for British MBA students because it was deemed to have a 'strong culture'. The fact that its culture was inflexible didn't seem to worry anybody at the time, least of all its managers, who were riding high on a seemingly inexorable rise in sales. Unfortunately, none foresaw the confluence of competition, demographic realities and lifestyle trends that would lead the company almost to ruin in only a few years, and the shareholders eventually had to install a specialist corporate celebrity, Stuart Rose, to turn things around.

As we discussed in Chapter 2, corporate adaptability depends on scenario-building – determining how your industry will look in the future based on the likely convergence of incipient trends, and painting a picture of how your organization will fit into that future to enthuse your staff. It's a skill that is becoming increasingly important not only to CEOs but also to middle-managers, whose input is essential to predicting the future role of individual business units within organizations and supply chains. However, the ability and willingness of middle-managers to think long-term on behalf of their companies is no longer guaranteed, given the increased unpredictability of their career paths. The job tenure of CEOs is now down to three or four years, while the company tenure of managers is around seven. In both ranks, interims will increasingly have to be used to enable employers to manage continual change. In a 2005 survey, according to Cantos (a consultancy), nearly one in five chief executives in FTSE 100 companies were churned and one in three of the present incumbents have been in their jobs for less than two years.

In the coming decades, no single team of permanent managers will have all the skills and experience needed to face every possible challenge. Already, very few managers are sufficiently skilled and versatile to respond to their companies' changing needs. Nevertheless, many Western companies in the service industries still give new recruits inflated expectations of advancement, clinging to the outdated notion that a guaranteed career path exists. And many others continue to recruit new managers based on qualifications and experience that do not guarantee the skills necessary to cope in a flexible, informal environment (for example, soft skills such as empathy). In the past, companies could fall back on the talents built into their permanent management structure, but in an era of rapidly shortening product life cycles and increasing global competition, that structure needs to be continually renewed. Exploiting new territories, trends or technologies will increasingly be beyond permanent managers while requiring more in-depth attention than the sort provided by management consultants. Today, interims occupy a minority of management positions; in the future, they could occupy the majority.

Large companies will, in particular, need corporate travellers with strong leadership skills – leadership interims – to run self-contained project on indefinite timescales. They will also need these interims within their leadership core if sufficient levels of flexibility and adaptability are to be maintained. Meanwhile, small companies will increasingly bring in interim managers to assist with particular projects, perhaps related to periods of growth and change in new territories, in the same way that many have used non-executive directors for specific development stages in the past.

Clearly, this will create new leadership challenges: how, for example, will companies generate commitment and engagement amongst staff who are strategically indispensable yet regard their tenure as fixed and short-term? To be successful, any pro-gramme of change has to embraced by managers at every level; otherwise their pervasive leadership will be half-hearted and opportunities will be missed. It is the job of the corporate celebrity to make newcomers enthusiastic about the cause and appreciative of how their role contributes to broader goals. Equally, financial and quality-of-life incentives must be intro-duced to substitute for guaranteed career prospects, orderly promotion and share options. Ultimately, companies will have to forge long-term strategic partnerships with interim management agencies in the same way they already deal with, say, component suppliers. These agencies will themselves become corporate ele-phants or entrepreneurial fleas, specializing in particular indus-try sectors, company development stages and geographical regions. So, for example, the resurgent wave of start-ups in Silicon Valley should be able to use interim managers to prevent a repeat of the 1999–2000 dotcom crash; indeed they may find that the use of interim managers is a condition imposed on them by their backers.

The growth of interim management is also being fuelled by changing attitudes among managers themselves: fewer and fewer now want long-term careers in companies, even if these are available. Instead, they want change, challenge, excitement – work they find personally fulfilling. They don't want to be accountable to line managers except on a short-term basis. Already, they think of their lives as a series of projects, in terms of both home and work. Interim management offers them a model of work that is entirely compatible with this ambition.

Are leaders born, or are they made?

Higher education in the West is still so bureaucratic and skewed towards mass markets that it is standardizing views and values. In the eyes of major recruiters, it is producing potential corporate lieutenants and stalwarts rather than the leaders so desperately needed, with qualifications bearing little relation to suitability for leadership roles. Accordingly, blue-chip companies are once again attaching a high premium to attendance at elite universities – institutions that have a tradition of nurturing individuality and initiative. Many will consider only candidates from Harvard, the US Ivy League colleges and a few others such as Oxford, Cambridge and INSEAD and reject the rest. This new elitism is based on social and emotional as well as intellectual capabilities rather than privilege; nevertheless, it's compounding a two-tier higher education system that will only be rectified if lower-performing universities take steps to identify and nurture the creativity, soft skills and initiative of their students required by their future employers.

Strong leadership skills are not the preserve of the intellectually gifted. Many of the most successful entrepreneurs in the world are college dropouts or self-educators who 'learnt on the job'. Therefore, recruiters need to be more appreciative and tolerant of the non-certificated features in someone's background that can signal leadership potential. For example, a gap-year between school and university spent travelling internationally could be evidence of broad cultural experience, while demanding personal interests could demonstrate abilities such as self-confidence, team-working ability and other soft skills.

Moreover, leadership skills can be nurtured within the organization. Traditional methods of management development can identify strengths and weaknesses, while simply throwing someone with potential into a challenging situation is a tried-and-tested way of bringing out their leadership skills. Install them in a part of the organization where they have little experience; give them tough situations to sort out; put them in charge of a subsidiary company or even a joint venture abroad – at the very least they'll develop a distinctive skill-set, a potential source of the admiration described above.

As for internal or outsourced executive training, its approach will have to be more far imaginative in future, helping potential leaders to develop personal qualities – the means to generate admiration, inspiration and trust – that their higher education probably neglected, as well as preparing them for increased cultural diversity. In particular, providers of MBAs must shift their emphasis from raw management skills to leadership qualities, while becoming increasingly international in outlook. Some business schools are already putting greater emphasis on developing social and emotional intelligence, but they are still largely bureaucratic, slow to adapt and stifling to creativity.

Endnotes

1 The idea factory: Technology giant 3M, based in Minnesota, United States, is widely regarded as one of the world's most innovative companies. This is not simply because it has over 55,000 product lines, or because it has access to the best brains and equipment, or even because it has processes in place to 'collide' previously unrelated technologies, in the belief that the best ideas result from interdisciplinary friction. No, 3M's secret weapon is that, for over half a century, it has recognized the need to encourage personal initiative. In 1948, former chairman William L. McKnight described his management ethos as follows: 'As our business grows, it becomes increasingly necessary to delegate responsibility and to encourage men and women to exercise their initiative. This requires considerable tolerance... Mistakes will be made. But if a person is essentially right, the mistakes he or she makes are not

as serious in the long run as the mistakes management will make if it undertakes to tell those in authority exactly how they must do their jobs. Management that is destructively critical when mistakes are made kills initiative. And it's essential that we have many people with initiative if we are to continue to grow.'

5 Young Asia meets the Old West: key demographics will change your markets

The global timebomb

- The affluent spenders of India make it a bigger consumer market than Europe by 2020
- If it's China today, India tomorrow?
- Europe can only compete with inward migration – time to get positive
- Western populations are getting older but behaving younger
- Countries of single people demand new marketing and selling approaches
- Workplaces of single men and women – get ready HR specialists

The demographics of India and China are daunting to those of us in business elsewhere in the world. In terms of sheer population size, they seem destined to hold an unassailable advantage over other economies.

Given the recent performance of India and China, it almost seems possible that they could achieve such growth. On a purchasing power parity (PPP) basis, they accounted for 32 per cent of global GDP growth in 2003. And, as we discussed in Chapter 1, they will be in third and first place respectively in the GDP world ranking by 2050. Yet it's important to remember that, while Asia may have more human resources than any other region in absolute terms, its growth potential depends largely on how those resources are developed. Business competitiveness is directly comparable to sporting competitiveness in that, to achieve success on a global scale, a country requires more than simply a deep pool of talent from which to draw its stars.

Yes, Asia's demographic changes will affect Western business more than any other trend in the coming decades. But as we've discussed, this will create just as many opportunities as threats. Already, the West is benefiting dramatically from the deflationary influence of Asian manufacturing, made possible by their huge workforces, who are grasping alternatives to agrarian poverty for the first time. Similarly, Western companies are beginning to find valuable new markets among the growing middle classes of India and China, which are already large in absolute terms in spite of the fact that they represent only a small proportion of their domestic populations. One-half of the population of India lives on less than US $1 a day. It follows that the growth potential for middle-class spending in both countries is vast, and since Western companies are highly experienced in providing consumer products and services, they should have a competitive advantage against home-grown companies in Asia.

Moreover, company leaders in the West shouldn't focus so hard on the rise of India and China that they lose sight of demographic changes at home that will also have a profound influence on their future growth prospects. We all know that our ageing populations are creating huge burdens for the future, but they are also creating valuable new markets.

Moreover, as we'll discuss in detail below, the number of single-person households in the West is growing dramatically, with a corresponding increase in demand for certain household and lifestyle products and services.

Finally, it's important for Western companies to compare the demographics affecting their own countries with incipient trends in Asia. Countries such as India and China may be

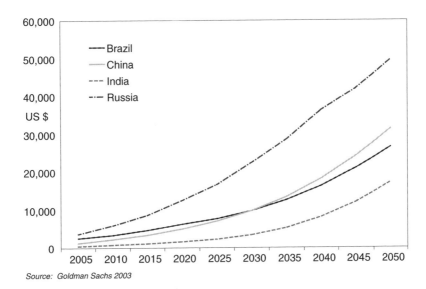

Source: Goldman Sachs 2003

Figure 5.1 Projected GDP per capita to 2050

young and vibrant now, but they too will eventually experience the same or similar demographic patterns as their populations grow more prosperous and older. If you can adjust successfully to the demographic challenges of the West today, you should find it easier in the long term to adjust to the demographic challenges of the East.

People power: why Asia's population trends are everyone's business

India and China aren't just big, they're big in the right places – together they account for about a third of the world's population, and a staggering 40 per cent of its total working population (that is, people aged 15–64). As the United States and Europe lose more and more workers to retirement, Asia's workforce is set to be replenished for the next few decades at least by healthier birth rates. According to UN estimates, the compound annual growth rate (CAGR) of India's population will be 0.9 per cent in the period 2000 to 2050, compared with a figure of 0.2 per cent in China.

India's working population is set to overtake that of China around 2035. It has a much higher number of English speakers than China, making it an attractive offshoring destination for Western service companies, but it also has a much higher illiteracy rate – around 40.5 per cent compared with China's 9.1 per cent. Moreover, China has done a much better job at creating huge employment for its unskilled workers via the new urban private sector, by investing heavily in infrastructure as well as loosening its grip over industries that were previously controlled by the state. Its cities have thus drawn in millions of workers from the impoverished countryside. By comparison, India is flagging – around 58.5 per cent of its workforce is still dependent on agriculture, compared with an equivalent figure of 45 per cent in China.

In the coming decades, we can expect to see both countries investing heavily in areas where they are currently deficient. So, for example, China will be trying to attract more services business by improving its management quality and encouraging its companies to pursue joint ventures with Western equivalents. Thanks to its present investment in high-tech clusters and higher education, it should be in a good position by 2010–15 to begin competing with India for deals in IT services and business process outsourcing. Meanwhile, India will be focusing on manufacturing, with a view to lifting many more of its rural workers out of poverty in the way China has done so successfully. It is therefore likely to offer some very attractive opportunities to Western companies for production offshoring, while consolidating and expanding its ability to support service companies abroad.

Good, bad and ugly trends in the Old West

Meanwhile, in the West, the populations of most countries are ageing rapidly. From 2010 onwards, its 'age dependency' (the number of non-workers expressed as a percentage of the working population) will rise sharply. In the United States, this proportion will rise from around 50 per cent today to a peak of over 60 per cent around 2035, while in Western Europe it will rise from 50 to around 75 per cent over the same period. In other words, there will be a huge number of elderly people expecting support from a dwindling number of young people, whose numbers are not going to be replenished fast enough owing to low or even negative birth rates.

The United States

No other developed country in the world will match the United States for population growth in the coming decades. The Land of the Free is super-sizing at a rate of 1 per cent a year, which means its present headcount of 300 million will reach 450 million by 2050. Why the surge? Because American women give birth to two children each, on average – far more than their European sisters – and because around 1.2 million seekers of the American dream immigrate into the country every year.

The United States isn't quite the Peter Pan economy of the West – like most other developed countries, it will see its average age rising sharply after around 2010. However, it will have a higher proportion of young people for longer, and that means its economy, especially the consumer goods industries, will continue to be driven by youth preferences and tastes. Hollywood, the *de facto* custodian of the US 'brand', will continue to lead the country's media in the export of youth-oriented entertainment. However, the marketers of US consumer brands will increasingly find that the hip-and-trendy strategies they use at home are inappropriate to the demographic profiles of Western Europe. If they wish to maintain growth amid ageing populations, they'll have to adapt their messages. But why should they bother when they can achieve much higher growth for much less effort by shifting their focus to the markets of India and China? In the coming decades, you should expect to see their product and service portfolios adopting a distinctly Eastern flavour.

More than ever, the United States needs a cosmopolitan attitude, not only to seize growth opportunities in the world's newly opening markets, but also because demographics at home are creating a far more multicultural society. In particular, the Hispanic population of the United States is burgeoning – it will triple in size by 2050 to represent about a quarter of the country's total population. Over the same period, the Asian population will triple too, to reach 8 per cent of the total. Non-Hispanic whites, meanwhile, will see their proportion decline from 70 to 50 per cent.

The United States is about to enter an extended period of diversification – in its consumer goods, as the tastes of different cultures disrupt traditionally dominant brands, and in its services, which will need additional language skills to give them a competitive advantage. The best spoils over this period will go to companies that best serve the Hispanic communities along the eastern and western seaboards, or who find ways to cater for specific tastes and needs among ethnic groups such as second-generation migrants from places such as Mexico. Ultimately, the growth of Hispanic entrepreneurship will be crucial the growth of the United States as a whole.

The biggest contributing factor is the gender revolution: as women have shaken off their traditional domestic roles, pursued higher qualifications and full-time careers, so a growing number have chosen to defer motherhood. In the UK the average woman used to have her first child at 22–3, now she has it at 28–9, and regards her maternity leave as nothing more than a career interlude. The same is the case in the United States and Northern Europe. What's more, an increasing number are choosing to have no children at all in order to preserve their work/life balance – if both members of a couple have careers and aspirational lifestyles then their self-fulfilment may override the desire to saddle themselves with children. Indeed, recent rises in house prices mean that many women feel they can't afford to take the time off work to have children and still pay their mortgage.

The United Kingdom and Ireland

Judging by its low birth rate (an estimated 11.34 births for every 1,000 people in 2002), you'd be forgiven for thinking that the UK has no need to worry about overpopulation. Not so. In the coming decades, the question of where Britons choose to live is going to have a serious impact on the social fabric of the country and its business prospects.

The UK's total population is set to remain static or even decline slightly, yet by 2020 it will need 24 million new homes, an increase of 25 per cent since 1991, to occupy the same (small) space. Why? Because of the increased number of people living alone – 40 per cent of UK households will consist of single people by 2016. What's more, this increased demand for housing will be focused largely in the southern part of the country. The population of London is predicted to grow by 800,000 to 8.1 million, a rise of 10.67 per cent, between 2006 and 2016.

The seeds of this imbalance were sown during the Industrial Revolution, when the UK concentrated its industrial power among the uneducated masses of the north and London thrived as a trading hub, consolidating its political, cultural and intellectual power. Then, during the 20th century, the city's financial district built on its reputation as a cluster for international finance to become the engine of the UK economy as manufacturing declined. Today, the south-east of the country is the natural home of the UK's knowledge-based businesses, while the north is struggling to define a new vision of growth for itself. The increased mobility of companies in the knowledge economy has compounded this problem since it is now just as easy to situation a business unit in India or China as in Scotland or the north-east of England. These regions badly need to differentiate themselves and, in places, foreign direct investment (FDI) has been courted specifically for this reason – for example in the call-centre cluster centred on Glasgow. However, at present, it seems that only a prohibitive cost of living around London will be able to check its progress.

House prices have rocketed across the UK in recent years but especially in the south. London's growth has obviously created a need for more so-called 'key workers' in the public sector such as nurses, social workers and teachers, yet no one in these sorts of jobs is able to get a foothold on the local property ladder. And even if enough new land was found to satisfy housing demand in both the public and private sectors, there would be other serious problems to overcome, such as a dwindling water supply. The UK government needs to take some courageous long-term decisions. If it fails to do so then London and UK business as a whole must prepare for increased social and economic turmoil.

By contrast, the Republic of Ireland is the only country in the European Union (EU) to have experienced a significant population increase in recent years, which should help sustain the spectacular growth it has seen over the past 15 years. The Celtic Tiger is creating far more jobs at present than Northern Ireland – its educated, English-speaking and relatively cheap labour makes it an attractive offshoring destination for UK companies, and it is very active in terms of entrepreneurship, producing 2,000 new businesses a month in 2004. (In the same year, it was ranked seventh for 'Total Entrepreneurial Activity' out of the 22 countries in the Organization for Economic Co-operation and Development (OECD).) Having English as its predominant language has also helped Ireland to attract FDI, although the improved stability in Northern Ireland has won much foreign capital too in recent years, especially from Irish communities in the United States.

The rest of the European Union

Such trends are increasingly influencing the political agenda of the EU, especially in Scandinavia, which has the most family-friendly policies in the world in terms of maternity and paternity leave, as well as a high degree of protection against gender discrimination. Elsewhere, governments are taking action to arrest the population decline. In France, for example, the government has intervened to increase the birth rate by introducing a raft of family-friendly policies, designed to improve childcare facilities and promote work/life balance. However, it is very difficult to balance the need for such initiatives with the need for competitiveness in a global economy dominated by Asia. As this book goes to press, France looks poised to drop its adherence to the 35-hour working week, which has been blamed for a decline in productivity. And the average EU birth rate of around 1.48 children per woman doesn't look like rising any time soon, even though a figure of 2.1 children per woman is required to replace the working population without immigration.

Clearly, this will have a massive impact on economic growth – in the European Union, for example, it is estimated that growth could drop from around 2.2 per cent in 2006 to 1.3 per cent in 2031–50. A former EU commissioner from the Netherlands, Frits Bolkestein, recently suggested that this stagnation would call the long-term survival of the euro into question. In any event, it will put massive pressure on pension funds, healthcare systems and housing – the longer you live, the more likely you are to live alone, and to suffer from disabilities. Another trend compounding these problems is the increasing number of people choosing to retire early, typically in their 50s. Many are exhausted casualties of the performance targets now used by most Western companies, while others have simply worked hard to buy themselves a leisurely existence. As far as many of the baby-boomer generation are concerned, work is something to be endured only until you can afford your ideal lifestyle.

Retirement has been redefined. It's no longer a waiting period for death but a time when you can stop 'wasting' your time doing work and start realizing your ideal lifestyle. In other words, it's time to spend some serious cash: the new big spenders in lifestyle sectors such as dining, travel and fashion are the over-50s. In the UK, according to the British Household Panel Study, those in the 50s age group are spending an increasing amount of their income on leisure and entertainment: 32 per cent of this age group spend over £50 a week on leisure activities, 25 per cent spend a similar amount on eating out and 28 per cent go out for a drink at least once a week. These figures are not noticeably different from younger age groups – in fact, the spending patterns of younger and older consumers are converging. The saying

'Life begins at 50' is now, for many people, sincere rather than sarcastic. As their life expectancy has increased, so people's view of certain ages has changed irrevocably; after all, if you can expect to live to nearly 80 then you will have a very different view of your 50s from that of your parents. Perhaps the most dramatic consequence is that an increasing number of people in their 40s and 50s are getting divorced, having retired early and realized they no longer like the idea of spending their remaining decades with each other.

The increased churn of relationships is not just a middle-aged phenomenon, of course. Westerners of all ages are ditching old partners and finding new ones more frequently than ever before. Our idea of youth is being extended in line with longer lifespans and a media culture that is still predominantly youth-oriented. As a result, we're spending additional years exploring possibilities – material, professional and emotional – thereby exercising the innate rights of young people everywhere. We're also becoming relationship consumers, shopping around for our ideal partners and not feeling under too much pressure to find them unless we feel a particular impulse to have children. Parents and their children can now split up at the same time, with people in their 50s just as concerned to make a new relationship work (and to spend the same amounts of money) as people in their 20s. This was among the trends dramatized by the hit US TV show *Sex & The City*. When the show finished its six-year run in 2002, the youngest of its four female stars was 38 and the oldest was 48 – in fictional terms, they had each lived the dream of the US urban elite, one of personal and material fulfilment followed, in the nick of biological time, by the discovery of life partners.

It follows that any company serving the supposed 'youth' market can now extend the life of its products and services. Sectors such as health, beauty and fashion can now find customers of almost any age. Research shows that people in the West don't feel old until they're 60, when lifestyle spending shifts away from relationship management and into more sedentary pursuits such as home furnishings, gardening and travel. Moreover, the age-related trends that have taken decades to become significant in the West are likely to become significant in the East far more rapidly. In India and China, the young urban elite are already using their newfound prosperity to mimic Western lifestyles through conspicuous consumption. Their wider populations may be ageing slowly, but you can bet they too will be influenced by their Western peers, and will expect to take advantage of the opportunities just as rapidly as they have seized their recent economic growth.

Why mass migration needs a rebrand

Most countries in the West are either going to have to raise their birth rate dramatically in the coming decades or rely on inward immigration to provide them with the skills and bodies they need. It's in the interests of both public- and private-sector organizations to help assimilate workers with foreign backgrounds, and to develop their leadership and management skills to handle the increasingly multicultural business environment.

Ask the average Westerner how their government should respond to the prospect of increased immigration and they are likely to mention burdens on social services, urban housing and general social unity. Those in authority – including politicians, the media and business leaders – must therefore do their part to foster cultural pluralism and draw the indigenous population away from divisive, exclusive and prejudiced tendencies. It's true that a growing immigrant population will create pressures on housing, with careful civic planning required to prevent the formation of enclaves, and instead set up balanced, inclusive and affordable neighbourhoods. Yet an indigenous population can have the idea of extra immigration 'sold' to them if it is made sufficiently clear that immigrants will help to alleviate the burden on state welfare systems and enrich the local economy.

In the coming decades, the public sector will have to redouble its efforts to help immigrants improve their language skills; their general skills in literacy and numeracy; and even specialized skills if these will help plug specific shortages or contribute to local clusters of expertise and entrepreneurship. Yet private-sector companies will also come under increasing pressure from their governments to aid the social integration of their immigrant employees. HR departments should in any case be developing their skills in cultural harmonization, as companies spread themselves across more countries than ever before. The benefits of providing immigrants with language training in the workplace are obvious to employers; what's less obvious but no less valuable to everyone is the use of such activities to promote understanding between different nationalities and ethnic groups. Local authorities will increasingly have to form strategic alliances to integrate companies with their local communities.

Independent living: the West's most influential export

'Hell is other people,' said French philosopher Jean-Paul Sartre. It seems that an increasing number of Westerners agree, as far as their living arrangements are concerned. Where cohabitation

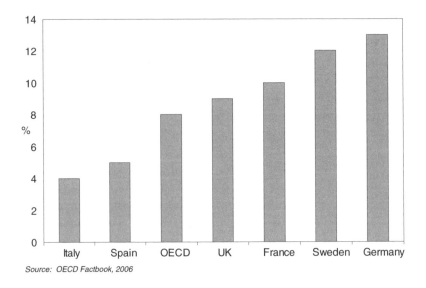

Source: OECD Factbook, 2006

Figure 5.2 Foreign born as a percentage of total population circa 2000

used to be a financial necessity and a social convention beyond a certain age, it is now a matter of preference for affluent young professionals. As far as they are concerned, self-actualization is predicated on personal and professional development, career progress and the purchase of tasteful products and services. They certainly don't need a co-dependent 'other' to make them feel complete – at least, not until infirmity beckons.

You can see this attitude clearly at work in the UK. Here, the following social changes are predicted to take place between 1991 and 2011: a 4 per cent decline in married couples, a 27 per cent increase in cohabiting couples, a 33 per cent increase in lone-parent households, and a 55 per cent increase in single-person households. By 2016, over 40 per cent of UK households will be occupied by married or cohabiting couples while a similar proportion will be occupied by just one person.

The dominance of live-alone men and women households is already evident in the major cities of the world, including Stockholm, New York, Los Angeles, Berlin, London, San Francisco and Amsterdam. The business opportunities this will create are massive: the greater the total number of households,

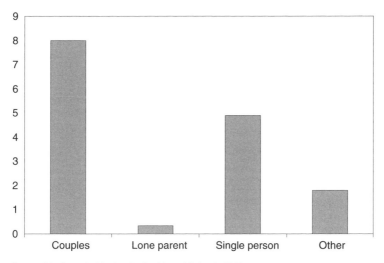

Source: Joint Centre for Housing Studies, Harvard University 2006

Figure 5.3 Changes in US household types 2005–15 (millions)

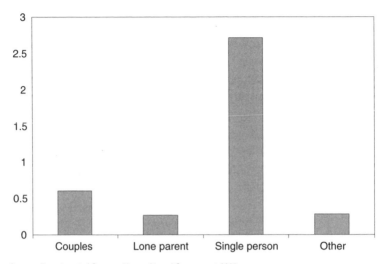

Source: Department of Communities and Local Government 2005

Figure 5.4   Changes in UK household types 2003–26 (millions)

the greater the number of duplicate goods required to serve them, especially in categories such as white goods, home-improvement supplies, fabric and furnishings. It will also create a boom in the number of small consultancies offering highly personalized lifestyle services – from interior design and fashion advice to personal fitness training and nutritional advice. Equally, the retail and marketing arms of larger companies must adjust to the fact that purchasing decisions are made increasingly by individuals rather than by couples and family units.

Meanwhile, the rise of independent living is creating big social challenges for national governments and local authorities. Single people have very different housing requirements from those of couples and families – they want to be where the action is, in urban areas, near to good communications and amenities, with as much pleasant ambience and security as they can afford – and this increasingly means social polarization, in places where the affluent choose to live in gated communities, sequestered behind tall fences and manned gatehouses. This pattern is clear in many of the inner-city regeneration programmes in New York, London and Copenhagen.

Demand from single young professionals is leading to the regeneration of many inner-city areas across the West. If you want to live within easy access of work and the best amenities, you'll probably be willing to pay a premium for new-build property on brown-field land, and even more for reconditioned industrial property with its high ceilings and 'rustic' exposed beams and brickwork. It's a principle that property developers have turned into cash ever since heavy industry began its wholesale shift to Asia, leaving acres of inner-city property vacant in former factory zones and commercial docklands. Buy up the property cheaply, persuade the local authorities you will help to regenerate the area in return for residential planning permission and improved communications and voilà! It's a millionaire-making process that has been copied from Copenhagen to Hamburg and Los Angeles to Leeds. Whether this can truly be called 'regeneration' is another matter – any area will benefit from an influx of wealthy people, but only if they spend their money in the local area rather than simply regarding it as a well-connected dormitory. Local authorities in areas that are ripe for conversion need to keep a tight rein on planning permission in the coming decades, to ensure that their civic planning is balanced and not overly geared towards residential development.

What liberation and loneliness mean for business

Today's single young professionals feel more socially and professionally mobile than their predecessors, but they also know that they inhabit a world in which jobs can be as transient as lifestyles. Consequently, many feel vulnerable and insecure, and most are on a constant search for meaningful relationships. The past few decades have seen a boom in newspaper personal ads, online dating agencies and networking websites. Online chat rooms, e-mails, weblogs, text and photo messages, cheap international telephone calls – all these things have diminished the amount of physical contact in the average human relationship, in the developed world at least. Tens of millions of people worldwide even have second identities that inhabit virtual environments known as 'massively multiplayer online role-playing games' (MMORPGs). Advanced networking technologies are making it easier for us to find others based on highly specific personal preferences and shared interests, but they don't guarantee the honesty of strangers, and they can't guarantee the geographical proximity of those we find appealing.

All this has major implications for spending patterns, which fluctuate wildly in line with personal circumstances. There's a big difference, for example, between consumers who have been living alone for some time and those who have just separated.

Personal relationships, like work relationships, are becoming more transient – young people tend to go through partners much faster these days, and divorce rates in most Western countries are high. One of the social categories showing a big increase in single-person households at present is the 30–60 age range. Middle-aged women especially are choosing to live alone, free of the social stigma of the past, protected by improved alimony laws and confident of social mobility in a way that their relatively uneducated ancestors never were. Recent health studies have suggested that a woman becomes more unhealthy and sad if she lives with a man, while, for the man, cohabiting has the opposite effect.

The other catalyst to the growth of single-person households is increased life expectancy. Historically, the majority of elderly people living alone were women, but now that men are living longer they are also increasingly living alone, too. One contributing factor here to this trend is that early retirement extends life expectancy. If you retire at 65 you'll probably be dead by 70, but if you retire at 60 then you'll probably live until you're 80. Why? The reason is that people who work until 65 are often in low-income jobs that contribute to ill health, and are more likely to have an unhealthy lifestyle involving smoking and lack of exercise.

Admittedly, age is no longer the obstacle to fresh romance that it once was. In the past, individuality died once you passed a certain age, and with it any realistic hope of being picked off the shelf. Now there's a growing category of older men and women who are concerned about their appearance and keeping fit – cosmetic surgery, grooming products and health products tailored to middle-aged people are booming. As we'll discuss further in Chapter 6, the traditional market segmentation of many mass retailers is becoming less meaningful.

Older single people are still effectively excluded from the types of places where the young go to meet new partners. And clubs and discos are no longer formal events at which to be introduced to a potential life-partner – they're thumping hot-houses where you can only meet someone at full volume. Many are finding that the internet can solve these problems, but those with low incomes and low levels of education are not equipped to use it. In particular, older men suffer from a total lack of support in this area, thanks to their lack of social skills.

Kissing the personal/professional divide goodbye

Most lasting relationships begin in the workplace – they always have done and they always will. In fact, office romance is set to reach boiling point in the West as the need for innovation breaks down traditional corporate structures in favour of close-knit teams, informal office layouts and prescribed socialization. The idea of keeping work and life separate or balanced is no longer possible for companies that wish to maintain a genuine competitive advantage. They need their employees to bond in the office, have fun together in the local pub and, if that leads to romance, so be it. Provided it doesn't adversely affect their work, of course.

Clearly, companies will have to be extremely careful in the way they attempt to control such tensions. If it's not clear where the boundary lies between work and personal relationships then the result may be a sexual harassment lawsuit. Equally, you can't legislate for personal feelings, and you'll only harm the creativity of close-knit teams by trying to intervene with ham-fisted policies. Most companies run away from such problems by calling for team dynamism while simultaneously maintaining their old, rigidly bureaucratic structures. The alternative is to provide adequate supervisory and advisory structures via the HR department to minimize inappropriate behaviour and potentially serious faux pas. You should also take a facilitative approach to resolving personal disputes or the emotional fall-out of failed relationships; if a problem arises that is affecting how one or more members of staff carry out their jobs then it will be reasonable for the company to find a sensitive way to arbitrate.

The flipside of a strong work-based social life is that it can be difficult for employees to make or maintain friendships beyond the company clique. Encouraging someone to socialize with their workmates can't be allowed to turn into emotional blackmail, under which individuals are judged harshly for detaching them-selves from team events. In particular, the voice of the single person must also be acknowledged more acutely in the company of tomorrow. Today, those who are unmarried, and especially those with no children, are commonly discriminated against in small but regular ways – typically by getting the last choice of dates on which to take their holidays. Also, in terms of the move towards 24-hour working, companies with family-friendly poli-cies often let down their single employees, because they are regarded as having no extra responsibilities.

All this is proof, if any were needed, that HR is a department of vital strategic importance. Spend enough time with the CEOs of today's highest-performing companies in the West and you'll find that they spend more time on HR than pretty much anything else. This is the experience of ex-GE CEO Jack Welch and it is confirmed by many others. They'll also ensure that their HR directors have a powerful position on the board. Why? Because they understand that optimal use of their people is the only thing that can counterbalance the cheap labour of India and China, and that the best way to disseminate their mission and vision in the knowledge-based economy is via a soft chain of command.

6 Hello to lifestyle tribes and what they can do for your business

---

We are liberated from our demographics

- The old get younger – and so do the young
- As consumers we are all full of contradictions
- Single men and women are the new big spenders
- Do we know 'who' we are?
- Lifestyle tribes are the new marketing categories
- Personalized customers expect personalized services – we are all celebrities now
- The attention-seeking 'look at me' culture

How many consumer categories can you name off the top of your head? If you're a marketer based in the West then the answer is probably dozens, if not hundreds. The amount of jargon used to describe market segments has shot up in recent years, and not only as the result of technical advances in marketing, corporate data-mining and 'customer relationship management' (CRM).

You may know the meaning of the term 'yuppie' (young, upwardly mobile professional), but how about 'yappie' (young, affluent parent)? The term 'dinkie' (dual income, no kids) has become widely used in recent years, but could your company be equally influenced by 'dumps' (destitute, unemployed mature professionals)? Some of these neologisms are invented for their comedy value but most are taken seriously by those whose job it is to identify groups of consumers at whom to aim new products and services.[1] Indeed, demand for them has never been higher – the number of consumer subcategories is rising fast, and will still be growing long after the clever nicknames have run out.

Recognizing potential customers was a far simpler business only a few decades ago. Back then, you could infer a great deal about an individual's spending patterns simply by looking at their age, occupation, income and gender. Today, these broad criteria are of limited use in isolation. In the coming decades, they will become less and less relevant to the way people see themselves; shape their identities and lifestyles; and spend their money. Even in developing economies, they mean a great deal less than they did during the less prosperous years of the West – thanks to the advance of communications and networking technology, the urban middle classes of India and China are already emulating the varied, category-resistant lifestyles of their Western peers. Furthermore, in countries where internet penetration is at its highest – and where most people grew up with a 'shop around' mentality, free to pick and choose from a variety of products and services – consumers are now highly sophisticated. They are, in effect, liberated from their demographic chains.

Why traditional market segments are past their sell-by date

Most companies still design and market their products and services to appeal to consumers in a specific age range of, say, '16 to 24' or '65+'. For those who make nappies, sell burial insurance or provide any other age-dependent product or service, this is clearly a vital approach. But for everyone else it's becoming a crude way to retain existing customers and attract new ones.

Consider for a moment the size of the age gap between your youngest and oldest customer. Has it widened in recent decades, with a similar average age but a more even spread in absolute numbers? If so, you may have started to divide your marketing into channels aimed at discrete age ranges. But have you really thought through the implications of the overall diffusion in your customer base? What your company and most others are witnessing is the erosion of links between demographic profiles and discrete life stages. It's a natural consequence of the demise of the traditional corporate hierarchy – no longer is age a guarantee of particular ranks or levels of remuneration. As the West has offshored its manufacturing facilities to Asia, so it has discovered that knowledge-work is especially prone to transience, uncertainty and risk. And as lifetime jobs are a thing of the past, so is the notion that certain jobs are appropriate only for certain ages. The marketers can no longer estimate with any real confidence how much money you have in your purse or wallet, nor what your earnings potential might be, on the basis of your age and occupation alone.

Compounding this problem is the wholesale shift in priorities among Western workers, away from cash and towards perks that enhance their quality of life. Increasingly, they are being rewarded not with extra pay or share ownership but with extra time off, flexible working hours, sabbatical leave or sideways transfers into positions that offer greater job satisfaction. All these situations have a massive impact on individual spending patterns, but none can be predicted using traditional market research techniques, locked as they are inside fickle minds.

It's true that companies are still greedy for their employees' time (the amount of unpaid overtime worked by the average UK employee was 7.4 hours per week in 2005, although this figure was down for the fourth year in a row). However, an increasing number are using free time as an incentive, and they recognize that in any case the boundary between free time and work time is increasingly blurred: most knowledge-workers can now negotiate to work outside the office for at least some of their allotted work time, provided they fulfil their duties and deliver results or projects on schedule.

Equally, in the West, we now take social mobility for granted so much that we're unafraid to start a new job or career at any age. We have redefined youth to the point where it can last into our 40s, and carry youthful attitudes with us into semi-retirement and beyond. This trend is partly the result of longer life expectancies and partly the result of a media industry led by the United States, with its comparatively young population. It doesn't mean that every marketing campaign should be youth-oriented in every location: Europe is, after all, becoming the old people's home of the world. But companies do need to acknowledge that older people are developing varied lifestyles.

Take the over-45s, for example. In the past, they were a conformist, conservative segment of society. Now they have interests and pursuits that are just as varied as those of their children. They include the first generation raised on consumerist principles, who aren't afraid to shop around in their professional lives or even their personal lives. Some have given up full-time jobs to become students or start businesses; others have replaced partners of 20 years with new ones; some are prepared to become

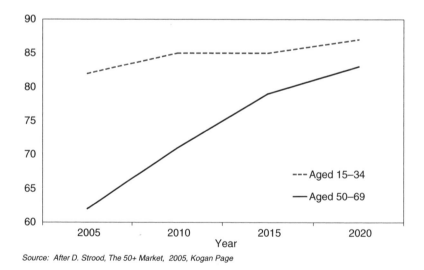

Source: After D. Strood, The 50+ Market, 2005, Kogan Page

Figure 6.1 Predicted numbers of US population aged 15–34 and 50–69 (millions)

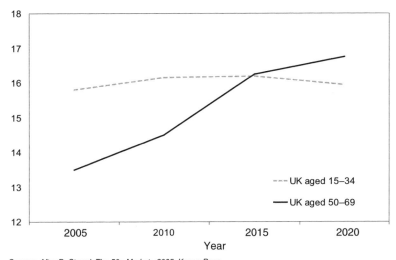

Source: After D. Strood, The 50+ Market, 2005, Kogan Page

Figure 6.2 Predicted numbers of UK population aged 15–34 and 50–69 (millions)

parents with new partners at the same time they become grand-parents. Transient relationships are now the norm rather than the exception, with many Westerners believing that a relationship commitment – whether or not it takes the form of a marriage or civil partnership – is probably only a medium-term arrangement at best. Thus the over-45s can – indeed must – be divided into a huge variety of subgroups: the remarried baby-boomers; the sandwich generation, looking after elderly dependants; the afflu-ent with no dependants; the financially strained with kids in college; as well as the traditional rose-tinted unit of the commit-ted couple.

From the corporate perspective, the increased number of single people at an older age means a significantly increased amount of spending on fashion, beauty products and other lifestyle purchases. If you're familiar with the range of cars made by Audi, you might think that most of its customers would upgrade from its TT sports car to a more practical saloon such as an A4 or A6. But in fact, many exchange models in the opposite direction. Why? Because many TTs are bought by middle-aged men who have just split up with their partners and want to trade in their A4s and A6s.

Why the world's big spenders
are now women

Business: it's a man's world, isn't it? You'd be forgiven for thinking so given the continued pay disparity between the sexes – in most countries. However, from the perspective of a modern marketer, the world's economy has been driven by women for some time, especially in the West. Their spending power has risen dramatically since the 1960s, in spite of the fact that equal opportunities legislation is clearly still being applied unevenly. At the same time, their control over household finances doesn't seem to have diminished. Today, in the average family unit, women make 93 per cent of all purchasing decisions and carry out 70 per cent of the shopping too.

Women also have a unique skill that marketers have only recently started trying to exploit, but that is quickly becoming vital to corporate strategies as traditional consumer categories disintegrate – the skill of networking. On average, men recommend positive customer experiences to 2.6 people, while women recommend them to 21 people. Why? Because women exchange information with friends, family, neighbours and work colleagues much more readily and effectively. Clearly, if a company gives its female customers a particularly good or bad customer experience, it has a disproportionate effect on their ability to attract new customers.

As far as spending patterns are concerned, women's personal preferences have also changed dramatically in recent years, in line with their increased independence and affluence. In this context, the two main effects of the gender revolution are: 1) an increase in the number of single or, at least, live-alone women, whose spending patterns have converged with single or live-alone men; and 2) the 'dinkie' household, which has a massive net income in comparison with that of newly-weds prior to the 1960s. The former is likely to spend heavily on beauty products, home furnishings and the duplicate items that every modern household requires, such as white goods; the latter is likely to spend heavily on support services such as childcare, cleaning and eating out.

For the moment, let's focus on the first category: the independents. Across the West, they're developing a much broader asset base through home ownership: a growing percentage of first-time mortgage applications in the United States and the UK are from single, live-alone women. This makes it imperative for companies who supply products such as furniture and white goods or services such as home security and maintenance to boost their appeal to women (notwithstanding the fact that women control the spending of shared households too). Already, the design of fast-moving consumer goods packaging and of many household items is becoming more feminine. However, the average shopping experience is still geared towards women who are part of family units, with a male partner and kids. In the future, retailers will need to ensure they can offer experiences that cater for the more assertive woman who has a strong career, an independent sense of identity and who probably lives alone.

In some Western cities, it is possible to find clusters of female-oriented shops and companies, including a high proportion of beauty salons. Single people have always been attracted to metropolitan areas, of course, but never before has there been a concerted effort on the part of retailers to establish zones of purely female-oriented commerce, in the same way that streets in parts of New York, Berlin and London developed exclusively to serve men's tailoring. In the coming decades, women will have their own, similar, points of geographical reference, whether these form spontaneously or as the result of deliberate efforts on the part of companies and local authorities. In particular, the beauty industry will continue to boom, in line with the elongation of perceived youth and the increased churn of relationships. Retailers also need to acknowledge that, as women continue to progress in the workplace, so they are likely to become much more time-impoverished.

Increasingly, they are shunning their tendency to browse and instead making purchasing decisions at speed – a key driver in the growth of online shopping.

Many companies have responded sensibly to the rise of women's purchasing power by adapting their products and services to appeal more effectively to female tastes, often hiring women to carry out this process. Nevertheless, most have yet to realize that they must reach out to subcategories such as single women, living on their own, from graduates in their early 20s to divorcees in their 40s or beyond. The convergence of male and female spending patterns in the West is not simply a matter of greater pay equality, it is a symptom of general confusion and insecurity over gender identities. Walk around the average North European city on a Friday night and you'll see 30-something women behaving like young men, where in the past they would have been curbing the young men's excesses. Importantly, the over-30s do not see themselves as middle aged. The diffusion of life stages and gender roles has led to widespread psychological insecurity, with adverse effects such as drink and drug abuse as well as the breakdown of traditional spending habits in other areas. Is it any wonder that, according to one recent survey, 91 per cent of women say 'advertisers don't understand us'?

The Me, Me, Me Generation: disoriented, desperate and disloyal

Westerners may be more prosperous than ever before, but they are also suffering from unprecedented levels of personal insecurity. Jobs for life, long-term relationships, traditional family forms and close-knit neighbourhoods all seem to be things of the past. Traditionally, these were the networks that gave us a source of security and that had a strong influence over our spending patterns. In the era before pervasive networking technology, peer pressure depended on physical proximity, and it was far more effective at generating conformity in lifestyles and corresponding expenditures. Today, the prevailing psychology in the West is one of transience in all things.

In the knowledge economy, companies feel more insecure and, as a result, so do their employees. The frequency of activities such as restructuring, mergers and acquisitions in recent decades has made it more difficult for the employees of large organizations to establish long-term social networks. Even the positive effects of free-market capitalism and globalization have, in some respects, compounded our sense of unease – the increased multiculturalism of cities, the increased cosmopolitanism of knowledge-economy jobs and the sheer volume of opportunity available to Westerners are all undoubtedly beneficial, but they are also bewildering. As physical and digital communications continue to advance, so we feel more and more compelled – indeed, pressured – to make full use of our freedoms.

Under these circumstances, most of us have naturally chosen to focus upon ourselves, continually asking the question: 'Am I getting the most out of life?' It's an attitude that has fuelled increases in early retirement, single-person households and relationship changes. Even members of committed couples increasingly think of themselves as individuals first and partners second. Westerners are spending more and more of their disposable income on the manufacture of identities – in other words, on self-indulgence, self-development and self-improvement.

This is not so much a matter of conspicuous consumption as of conspicuous personal presentation. Whether we are conscious of it or not, each of us is increasingly asking questions such as: 'How do I present myself in terms of my appearance, the lifestyle I choose to lead and the objects I choose to surround myself with?' Many companies already imply through their marketing campaigns that they can answer such questions. Industries such as beauty, fashion and home furnishing continually present us with visions to aspire to. Even holiday providers tantalize us with the prospect of experiences that are both enjoyable and enviable. Watch TV on Sunday and you'll see that all the commercial breaks are full of hair-care products. Why? Because it's at this time of the week that women feel most dissatisfied with their appearance after bad Saturday nights out. Marketing of this type is essentially in the business of fostering self-doubt, and it works in the West because our affluence persuades us that there is no need to wait for perfection.

In our pursuit of that modern Holy Grail, the 'ideal lifestyle', we're becoming ever more impatient, spurred on by a youth-oriented media that claims we can all achieve anything. As a result, we're making big decisions faster ('If I don't get the promotion I want then I'll immediately look for a job somewhere else!') and we're racking up huge personal debts as a result of our 'live now, pay later' mentality.

From the individual's perspective, it has become so natural and so easy to express individuality through lifestyle purchases that if we make no effort to do so then we are considered to be lacking in character. This is partly the result of the elongation of youth, since young people have always resisted conformity in an effort to define themselves, but it is also tied to the rise of 'celebrity' (as it relates to self-promotion, rather than to the superficial view that it can be a legitimate goal in itself). The good thing about the rise of celebrity culture is that it has demonstrated how free-market capitalism leads to social mobility – in other words, it has hammered the final nail into the coffin of traditional class systems. Few people now see themselves as members of a particular class, and a growing number feel that even occupation is insignificant to personal identity. The rise of the celebrity culture persuades us to act like celebrities in our individual networks, whether these are public or private, in order to be respected and admired. In our efforts to differentiate ourselves, we are becoming more self-obsessed. There is the emergence of the 'look at me' culture.

As we discussed in Chapter 2, celebrity culture is even penetrating the workplace, as Western companies try to find ways to optimize their human resources and compete with rivals in India and China. Corporate celebrities are forcing themselves to behave in passionate, charismatic and idiosyncratic ways to inspire employees, and employees at all levels are being encouraged to show their individuality as part of a general effort to foster innovation. The difference here, of course, is that the corporate celebrity depends totally on distinguished service and genuine achievement. It is a positive pervasive attitude for any company that wishes to stimulate creativity, and to nurture skills that allow formerly reticent individuals to build coalitions around great ideas. Acting like a celebrity at your company may well help you to win friends and influence people on social occasions, but it is (or should be) carefully circumscribed on company premises, and at times of customer contact or remote working.

Having said this, the constant pressure to reinvent and differentiate ourselves in the workplace is spilling into our identities as consumers to some extent. We have a growing tendency to repackage ourselves in different situations, and for many people this is raising nagging existential questions such as 'Who am I really?' and 'How do I establish my real identity?' In this context, it is easy to understand the growth of so-called 'new religions', which claim to offer a holistic explanation of who we are that is detached from the materialism, commercialism and branding of the modern world (notwithstanding the fact that these religions are in themselves brands with many of the same objectives as commercial organizations). Indeed, it goes some way towards explaining the increasing fundamentalism of old religions too.

The other question that Westerners are increasingly asking themselves – one that is arguably much healthier in view of its finite answers – is 'How do I acquire peace of mind?' For some, the answer is alcohol or drug abuse. For others, it is psychoanalysis or alternative therapy. But for most it is simply opting out of urban and corporate life, 'downshifting' or 'downsizing' to a house in the countryside, or simply living a lifestyle that is anti- or post-modern. Again, the implications for consumer spending patterns are huge and the ability of traditional marketing techniques to cope is questionable. Companies wishing to sell products and services to disoriented Westerners, and to the growing numbers of Asians experiencing *affluenza* for the first time, must categorize their customers based not on who they are but on what they want to be. In other words, they must learn how to identify, nurture and even create 'lifestyle tribes'.

What is a lifestyle tribe?

With all this talk of self-fashioning, it's easy to forget that we can have no identity of our own unless we affiliate ourselves with other people. This is the essence of the lifestyle tribe: an affiliation with people who share our interests and/or values, rather than any other attribute such as age, income, occupation, gender or even physical location. In the past, most people identified themselves according to the thing that gave them the most structure in their lives: their profession. If they were a member of a lifestyle tribe, it was as a secondary activity. First they were a bank manager, then they supported a baseball or soccer club. What's happening today is that affluent people are increasingly regarding themselves first and foremost as a member of a lifestyle tribe; if they do a particular job, it's simply because they need the money to support their membership of a lifestyle tribe.

Spotting dedicated members of a lifestyle tribe isn't difficult. They continually adhere to specific codes of conduct, dress styles and jargon. And some coalesce around corporate brands. Perhaps the best case study here is that of Harley Davidson, the motorcycle manufacturer, which has over 850,000 people in its 'fan club', a kind of extended after-sales service organization. Turn up to any Harley event and you'll find all the bikers decked out in similar clothing; meet them in any other context and you'll find they're teachers, bank managers and doctors... as well as heavy metal musicians. In the early 1980s, the company was in danger of losing its entire market to Japanese rivals. Today it has delivered almost 20 consecutive years of record sales and profits. The turnaround can be traced back to 1983, when Richard Teerlink took over as CEO and encouraged his senior managers to spend 10–15 days a year riding with customers, an initiative dubbed 'super-engagement'. At the time, the company's most loyal customers were fed up with the unreliable mechanics of Harley's bikes, the poor quality-control of its manufacturing and its non-existent after-sales service. Within a few years the brand's reputation had been restored and improved so much that it was able to sell everything from riding lessons and rentals to clothing and holidays.

Many other lifestyle tribes are based on obsessive hobbies, but in essence they all represent something more: a means for consumers to assume positive identities. Perhaps the most vivid are based on values – for example, animal rights protestors will very likely spend their money on vegetarian or vegan food, preferably organic, at retailers that either refute meat-eating or promote good animal husbandry, while eschewing cars in favour of public transport. It's a crude example but an instantly recognizable one, with corresponding spending patterns that are easy to explain. The problems start when you try to target products and services at, say, an oil futures trader who goes vegetarian and sells his Porsche to mollify his activist girlfriend, and then resumes his carnivorous, petrol-burning ways when they break up.

Other strong lifestyle tribes coalesce around sports teams such as Barcelona, Real Madrid, and the US-owned Manchester United, all of which have strong international brands that attract global-based lifestyle tribes; around sexually liberal communities, typically in the gay districts of the world's major cities with their clusters of lifestyle businesses; and around common pleasures such as food and wine. For decades now, Westerners have brought increasing numbers of exotic flavours home from their travels, created demand for them in supermarkets, and grown confident in how to make them in their own kitchens thanks to TV chefs. Now, for many, the pursuit of ever-greater delicacies for the taste-buds involves expensive utensils and ingredients, *cordon bleu* training and even more travel to gain experience and inspiration.

Elsewhere, lifestyle tribes that were previously strong are now in decay. Political parties, for example, are finding it difficult to recruit new members because they no longer seem to have values that are discernibly different from their rivals'. Equally, the 'country society' of the English upper classes or the metropolitan 'chic' of the United States is growing less meaningful as its ranks are infiltrated by *nouveaux riches*. In the past, the sports of hunting, game-shooting and polo – and the social scene that went with them – had such huge barriers to entry that they were completely inaccessible to anyone who didn't own land. But with today's social mobility, such exclusivity is less noticeable and less significant; today, lifestyle tribes cut across any such categorization. Madonna combines sexually explicit scenes in her rock 'n' roll stage sets with being the lady of the manor on her English country estate. They may have coalesced around sources of money in the past – as the yuppies did in New York City in the 1980s and the 'geeks' did around Silicon Valley in the 1990s – but modern communications and networking technologies mean they can find each other free of charge and free of the need to actually meet in person. 'Myspace' as online networking is a good example of this.

Just as the internet can enable companies to aggregate consumers with highly unusual preferences, so it can enable virtually any individual to find likeminded souls. If you can't spot these commercial opportunities then you shouldn't be in business. The highest-performing companies in the coming decades will be those that use networking technologies either to ensure they are serving the lifestyle tribes among their existing customers as well as possible, or to spot lifestyle tribes in which there is demand for their products or services, or to encourage the creation of new lifestyle tribes based around their brand(s). Ideally, they will do all three, and they will do it globally – even in developing companies, consumers can adopt the latest trends via the internet provided they have enough purchasing power.

In July 2005, Rupert Murdoch's News Corp. acquired Internix Media, the owner of networking website Myspace.com, for US $580 million. Why such a high price? Partly because of the raw numbers accessing Myspace every day – as of March 2006, it was the fifth most-viewed website in the English-speaking world. More significantly, over 10 million of its registered users regularly visit the site to update their own personal homepage, which lists huge numbers of personal preferences, includes a weblog facility and, in many cases, showcases photography or music. Each homepage also links to the homepages of 'friends'. In other words, this is a place where lifestyle tribes coalesce automatically. At the time of the acquisition, Murdoch said its primary benefit to News Corp. would be in the direction of traffic to the websites of Fox TV. However, its potential for advanced data-gathering and marketing is clearly enormous.

In addition, companies must monitor any lifestyle tribes they wish to serve – carefully, empathetically and continually – for signs of change. Today's consumers switch lifestyle tribes frequently and will often try two or more at the same time in the same way they might try on similar outfits in a store before handing over their credit card. And who can blame them when there are such a number of compelling alternatives to choose from – take a quick glance around the average newsagent and you'll find half a dozen magazines about sailing, a similar number dedicated to gardening (which used to be a hobby for the elderly and is now being promoted on the TV and in the print media by photogenic presenters as an exciting pursuit for the young) and hundreds about video games. The total number of consumer magazines has exploded in recent years because publishers have consciously created lifestyle tribes around hobbies and interests, in order to sell advertising space to, say, the designers of sailing apparel as well as boat-builders, and the manufacturers of garden furniture as well as plant-sellers.

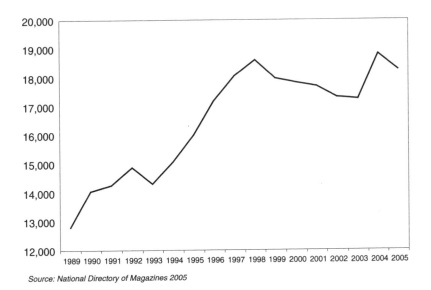

Source: National Directory of Magazines 2005

Figure 6.3 Number of US magazine titles 1989–2005

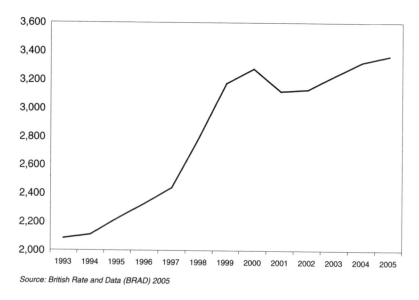

Source: British Rate and Data (BRAD) 2005

Figure 6.4 Number of UK consumer 'lifestyle' magazine titles 1993–2005

This last example is especially salient because homes are the places where people are most likely to reflect their affiliation with lifestyle tribes in terms of spending. In the past two centuries, the average home in the West has changed from being merely a base for sustenance and reproduction to being a base for entertainment (aka networking). As its material comforts have reached a plateau, so its owners have begun using it increasingly as a social setting, with architecture, furnishing and other status symbols arranged to reflect the owner's identity. In other words, they have copied the social practices that, previously, only the rich and powerful could entertain. The major difference is that modern, middle-class homes are increasingly designed to be convertible into places of work, with modular furniture and broadband internet connections that allow their occupants to take full advantage of any flexible working offered by their employers.

Of course, for those who are not affluent, educated or technologically literate, the age of lifestyle tribes promises to be a far lonelier place. If you have a limited sense of affiliation to any particular group as a result of unemployment or family disintegration, suffer from chronic illness or live alone in a run-down housing area then you probably won't be equipped to make friends online, and you'll certainly be ignored by marketers, as they become increasingly ruthless in their attempts to cut 'dead flesh' from the lifestyle tribes they wish to target and retain. The flipside of this predicament is that the internet could be tremendously helpful to such people in giving them a sense of belonging, not to mention returning them to work if they are able to do so. As we shall discuss in Chapter 7, regional and state governments will increasingly look to companies to help them bridge the technology gap and combat social polarization.

Born tribal: why ethnic minorities represent a huge growth opportunity

A particular form of lifestyle tribe is, of course, one based on non-indigenous ethnicity. Many companies in the West have realized in recent years that ethnic minorities represent a ready-made market for specialized products and services that will grow continually with inward immigration. As Western countries have become more multicultural, and as the tastes of their indigenous citizens have led to supermarket shelves being stuffed with foreign delicacies, so demand has grown among non-indigenous communities for products and services that reflect their unique lifestyle and place of origin.

For companies wishing to serve these markets, one of the main obstacles has been their disparate spread across urban centres. Traditionally, the only industry capable of connecting them was the media, with specialized publications, radio or TV channels. However, thanks to lean manufacturing, improved physical communications and the internet, it is now possible to aggregate them into significant markets. Furthermore, their spending power is increasing thanks in no small part to ethnic entrepreneurship (a significant and growing contributor to the GDP of the United States and many European countries). Research by

Barclays Bank in the UK shows that the number of Black and Minority Ethnic business start-ups has reached record levels. They have increased by around 33 per cent since 2000 and now account for 11 per cent of all start-ups. This is a similar pattern as in the United States where entrepreneurship is booming among minority groups. According to the latest US Census Bureau data the number of minority-owned firms now comprises more than 3 million. While US firms grew by 7 per cent, those owned by Hispanics and Asians increased by 30 per cent and those owned by African Americans by 25 per cent.

Like any other lifestyle tribe (or, indeed, any social network), an ethnic community will spread news of positive and negative customer experiences by word of mouth faster than artificial marketing ever could. What's more, it will respond favourably only to companies that show empathy as well as communication skills. This is particularly important in situations where a Western company successfully serves an ethnic minority in its domestic market, only to face competition from a foreign rival in the country where that minority originated. Indian and Chinese entrepreneurs in particular have the resources as well as the wherewithal to pull this trick. After all, it is now just as easy to send goods and information to Burnley from Bangalore as it is from Birmingham.

Can any marketing really get through to lifestyle tribes?

Given that lifestyle tribes are based on highly specialized tastes and requirements, doesn't that mean that going after them is solely an entrepreneur's game? Certainly, small and medium-sized companies will be in the best position to serve some lifestyle tribes, in situations where the mindset, culture and strategies of a large corporation are too inflexible and too removed from the marketplace to adapt and respond fast enough. Nevertheless, if your company has a transnational structure that is flexible and responsive then it should – if necessary – be able to use intrapreneurial cells or subsidiaries to serve numerous market niches profitably. You just need to establish the right procedures for collecting, mining and analysing customer data, so that your marketing department can distinguish the discrete identities your customers are fashioning for themselves, and the products and services this requires.

Many companies that deal in multiple products lines are already using customer data in this way – most notably supermarkets such as Wal-Mart in the United States and Tesco in the UK – via their loyalty card schemes. They're doing so chiefly to serve customers more effectively and steer them towards appropriate purchases – for example, through targeted special offers or even the rearrangement of products on the shelves to maximize the chance of impulse purchases. In the future, big retailers and other types of companies will increasingly collaborate to develop much more advanced models of lifestyle tribes, driving customers from store to store as well as from product to product, in order to maximize their spending. Such possibilities were undoubtedly one of the motivating factors behind the set-up of Nectar, a loyalty scheme operated by a UK consortium including Sainsbury, BP and American Express – it would take only the addition of a mobile phone service operator, with its ability to track the physical movements of customers, for this consortium to build a detailed profile of almost every moment of consumption in a person's life. Civil libertarians may be aghast at this kind of scrutiny, but there's no denying that it has the potential to lower prices across product and services classes on the basis of lifestyle tribe affiliation. More fundamentally, it could help to put offers in front of people that genuinely improve their lives, as well as the bottom lines of the companies they deal with.

Yet in spite of these developments, most companies in the West still continue to segment their customers by age, income, occupation and gender. Why? Because the rate cards of their sales people are printed with these categories, and because the traditional providers of customer data have a vested interest in the status quo. It is now possible to gather more information about customers than ever before, and in some respects to a higher quality, thanks to information and communications technologies – in particular, the proliferation of wireless devices, and their integration with purchasing systems, is leading to customer segmentation by IP address rather than postal address. However, you can't buy knowledge about niches off the peg. To identify and harness lifestyle tribes you need anthropological, qualitative research as opposed to demographic, quantitative research. More importantly, you need data collection and analysis based more on intuition, risk-taking and empathy, in concert with emotional research and human contact with the customer base – as Richard Teerlink found when he took off his suit, put on his leathers and rode out of Harley headquarters to meet his fans. In other words, you must convert your consumer marketing data into corporate strategic intelligence – something that software, in itself, does not allow.

First, you need to acknowledge that data-mining no longer yields broad trends from which you can develop entire portfolios. In the coming decades, its primary role will be to identify entrepreneurial opportunities, so that you can create internal hives of 'entrepreneurial fleas' to serve specific niches. Second, to draw people into a lifestyle tribe, you need feelers like an octopus to monitor tastes and exert subtle influence; and you need multiple price points that allow the maximum number of prospective customers to buy their way in. Finally, to nurture lifestyle tribes based on consumer goods, you ideally need to create a stepladder towards 'ultimate affiliation' – say, a set of clothes, accessories and technologies that marks the individual as a fully fledged affiliate – on which each rung is progressively more expensive. You can then work closely with advertising agencies to pull tribe-members gently upwards.

Overall, companies simply need to be more imaginative and specific in the way they market their products and services. It is the beginning of the end for most global advertising campaigns – why put all your eggs in one basket when consumers are increasingly fleeing from homogeneous offerings; recycling their possessions as they try on new identities; and boycotting brands whose values they find unacceptable? Global brands are becoming less significant to consumers than brands that are localized or linked to specific lifestyle tribes (a process that has been aided by the disaggregation of large corporate structures). After all, when you go to a supermarket to buy washing powder, do you look for the name Procter & Gamble or for one of its sub-brands such as Ariel, Bold or Tide? This will present a great challenge in the future for global (American) brands such as Coca-Cola, MacDonalds and Pepsi.

To guarantee growth in an age of lifestyle tribes, large companies will either have to create sub-brands that operate as independent, intrapreneurial cost centres or simply acquire smaller companies with localized or specialized brands in their portfolios. The latter is a time-honoured way to diversify, but it will need careful management in the future if the acquirer is to avoid accusations that it simply wishes to co-opt values it doesn't really believe. This criticism has been levelled recently at McDonald's in its acquisition of a controlling stake in the UK sandwich chain Pret A Manger, where each sandwich carries a label that reads: 'No factory, no shelf-life, made in-store, no "display until", no obscure chemicals'; and L'Oréal's recent acquisition of Body Shop.

Western consumers are highly distrustful of big business, big government and the media. We've become jaded after years of unfulfilled brand promises – especially those of us who are knowledge-workers, since we trade and work with our brains, are alert to every confidence trick in the book and are cynical about marketing messages that we find too simplistic. As a result, it has become difficult for companies with genuinely good products and services to reach us through conventional advertising – we simply no longer believe the hype. This is why companies are shifting from TV spot advertising to 'In Association' sponsorship, and product-placement in TV programmes and films. Smaller companies are actually benefiting from this disillusionment by using their size to give their customers much greater personal attention and/or marketing their products and services as 'authentic'. The key challenge for large companies in this context will be to prove that they can attach the same qualities to their superior economies of scale.

A related headache will be tracking the lifestyle tribes you are trying to serve, since they are always changing, and being adopted or abandoned by fickle consumers. Companies will have to be keenly aware of the overlaps between lifestyle tribes, to ensure they retain their existing customers or, if necessary, serve them in new ways through consortium arrangements. What's more, their competitive advantage will depend on how proactively they manage to do all these things. This is forcing customer relationship management (CRM) systems to adapt fast, even as their strategic importance is becoming greater than ever.

Move over CRM, here comes CMR (customer-managed relations)

The promise of CRM is to offer customers a consistent experience across all the functions of an organization, whenever they call customer services, meet a representative or make an enquiry in-store. Its ability to move information from side to side in an organization, rather than up and down traditional reporting lines, means that it can aid the process of corporate branding, delivering ever-changing, bolt-on packages of products to consumers. It can also establish profiles of past purchasing patterns that enable companies to start dividing their customers into categories for the purpose of improved service and marketing.

However, as consumers become more dynamic, so too must the way CRM handles data. In practice, it hasn't lived up to the hype it generated in the business press during the early 1990s. Sure, it can integrate a huge number of business processes, but it can't improve the overall performance of companies that are still rigidly hierarchical (ie the majority). Nor can it solve the problem of highly fragmented back-office activities, a growing problem as companies disaggregate into numerous trading units, profit centres and offshore operations.

CRM may allow for the processing of large amounts of customer data but, in itself, it cannot improve the quality of customer relations. In fact, in the longer term, it can have the opposite effect.

To begin with, most information gathered by CRM only reflects past purchases – without constantly renewed analytics, it's poor at tracking the fickle, experimental nature of modern spending patterns and at predicting what people are likely to buy in the future. In a sense, it brings companies too close to their customers, developing such a detailed focus on their present-day wishes that their future wants and needs are missed.

A further weakness of CRM in the retail sector is that the data it collects is based solely on products that customers have purchased in-store; by definition, it doesn't collect data on what customers decided not to purchase, even though this arguably has a more significant impact on the bottom line by – if nothing else – preventing inventory wastage. Did your customer decide not to buy something because it was poor quality or because they simply didn't see it on the shelf? Filling in blanks like this is becoming more and more vital to retailers in the fight for competitive advantage.

For CRM to be effective in the coming decades, it needs to shift away from technological dependence. The information it provides needs to be augmented with human contact – beginning with simple measures such as mandatory visits to the shop floor by store managers and senior executives, or regular conversation with customers and staff. It needs to be sprinkled with a layer of human intelligence and imagination. Information technology cannot displace the indispensability of these human qualities. If it does, the result is highly bureaucratized corporate processes that reinforce the distance between companies and their customers.

Moreover, CRM-based analytics will have to adapt to cope with the notion of aspiration in people's spending patterns; that is to say, they will have to account for the fact that an individual might be particularly frugal in one area of their life and exceed their budget in another, in order to affiliate themselves with a lifestyle tribe. The focus of all market research is shifting to the construction of mosaics, models that reflect the growing complexity of people's lives.

Finally, CRM will have to overturn its reputation as an invader of privacy. Western consumers are sick of providing personal information to companies in ever-increasing quantities. They regard CRM as gratuitous and inconvenient, particularly when customer databases are sold on to other companies or used by the same corporate brand to market other products and services. Customers don't want to be managed by companies, they want to manage their relationships with companies; in other words, what they want isn't CRM but CMR – 'customer-managed relations'. Traditionally we would walk past a shop, enter if we liked what we saw in the window and engage in negotiations. As the customer, we were in charge. With CRM, consumers are passive agents in corporate marketing and selling strategies. With CMR, the roles are reversed and there is a return to the historic relationship between purchaser and seller.

Having said this, putting control back into the hands of the customer will not be enough to ensure brand loyalty in the coming decades. As consumers become ever more sophisticated about using online technologies, so they will be ever more inclined – indeed, encouraged – to shop around, compare products and prices and then choose whether to purchase on- or off-line. Indeed, they may also be able to construct their own databases of preferred suppliers and, in doing so, play one off against the other. To hold on to them, you'll need to create a bond that is not only commercial but emotional.

Why consumers are increasingly spending from the heart

Across the West, and increasingly in affluent areas of Asia, consumers take it for granted that products and services will satisfy their everyday needs. They can be fairly certain, for example, that their vehicles and household appliances will not break down; that the food they buy in local shops will be prepared hygienically and will taste the way they expect it to; and that the services they pay for are adequately regulated and reliable. As a consequence, they are becoming less responsive to marketing that promises only material benefits. What more and more of them want to see in a potential purchase is an intangible quality such as a unique experience, an enhancement to their personal identity or a greater sense of affiliation to a lifestyle tribe. In essence, they want to be surprised – a tough challenge in a world of surplus where everyone has seen and bought it all.

The number of thrill-seekers in the world is rising rapidly, with extreme sports such as climbing, white-water rafting and bungee jumping enjoying huge growth. And, far from being the exclusive domain of the young, pursuits like these are, like so many others, now being infiltrated by men and women in middle age and beyond. From a financial perspective, this is not surprising given the rising number of older people who are still single and free of dependants, and therefore tend to have large amounts of disposable income. However, it overturns the traditional view that the young spend with their hearts while the old spend with their heads.

Westerners in particular seem to be so benumbed by consumerism that they are willing to pay through the nose for life-affirming experiences. Yet even they can be excited by products and services that are designed to elicit an emotional response as well as fulfilling their basic functions. Take the Apple Macintosh computer, for example – no matter which model you buy, the experience of owning it begins not with the start-up chime but with the opening of the box. Everything about the packaging and the ancillary parts of the device is designed to signal quality and to reinforce Apple's reputation for marrying form and function – look at any part of either the packaging or the hardware and you will see evidence of designers thinking to themselves: 'How can I make this look nicer?' The Apple lifestyle tribe is one that prefers to spend just a little more time, effort and money than its rivals in the interests of happiness. Indeed, Apple is so sure that its customers will be proud to be a part of its lifestyle tribe that it still gives away stickers of its logo with every computer.

Would your customers be proud to wear your logo? Would it make them happy to stick it above their desks? Probably not. Aside from the fact that Apple is one of only a handful of major companies to have successfully nurtured a lifestyle tribe, the 'brand faithful' are, in any case, on the decline. There used to be a correlation between brand loyalty and age: as you got older, so you became less experimental, and stuck with the brands you knew, in particular with types of products and services that were more onerous to switch such as cars or bank accounts. But this is no longer the case. All but the oldest Westerners have grown up with liberated consumerism, which means that, at all ages, they have experimental tastes and aren't afraid to shop around for good deals. Meanwhile, the 'brand detached' are on the increase. They're the disillusioned consumers who don't really believe in brands at all, who tend to purchase purely on the basis of price or quality. These liberated consumers are typically highly educated and use price-comparison websites as a matter of course. You might as well forget about them unless you're going to offer huge discounts or incentives.

Those in between could be called 'brand butterflies', people whose emotional loyalty to brands is transient, and who are always prepared to try out alternatives. Their influence has been felt particularly in deregulated industries where consumer disloyalty has been positively encouraged in order to break up former state monopolies – so, for example, in Scandinavia if you previously got your broadband internet connection from Telia then you'll be willing to try out Tele2, Telenor or some other provider. In this context, the rules of retention are being thrown out of the window. One of the most successful internet service providers in the UK in recent years, Zen Internet, has benefited hugely by actually rejecting the idea of minimum contracts – if you sign up for broadband with Zen then you can cancel the contract only a month later.

In the coming decades, companies wishing to grow will have to concentrate on retaining brand butterflies, and will have to show similar courage as they try to coax consumers without making them feel restricted. Clearly, this will make the collection, management and interpretation of data even more complex – it will take continual imagination and effort to collect and analyse psychological and emotional data from existing and potential customers. What's more, your marketing department will have to do more than simply boost aware-ness of your brand; it will have to boost its reputation. Indeed, this latter issue of status will arguably be more important – if you're trying to appeal to one lifestyle tribe rather than another, then you have to stand for particular values that arouse the emotions of its members.

Endnotes

1 Consumer acronyms: How many of the following do you recognize?
   - Hopeful – hard-up older person expecting full, useful life
   - Oink – one income, no kids
   - Rubbie – rich, urban biker
   - Scum – self-centred urban male
   - Sink – single, independent, no kids
   - Sitcom – single income, two kids, outrageous mortgage

7 The politics of tomorrow and what it means for business

Are national governments servants of corporate power?

- Business opportunities and high risk environments
- Corporate rip-offs in India and China
- The future for Africa is bleak
- A world of growing terrorism
- The fading 'brand' of the United States
- Achieving corporate social responsibility

The seemingly endless search for growth is taking Western companies into ever more risky environments. In the recent past, if they set up foreign operations it was generally in established market economies, with mature legal systems. Today, to survive let alone build a competitive advantage, they must set up complex collaborative arrangements with numerous foreign companies at high speed, often in places that are severely deficient in corporate, commercial and copyright law.

In this context, how do you protect your intellectual property (IP) and customer data? At present, the answer seems to be with difficulty. India and China both have underdeveloped IP laws and public records systems that make it difficult to conduct background checks on employees. If you're a software developer based in the West and you wish to take advantage of educated labour in India or China to carry out coding, then you can't fail to be aware that software piracy is an issue, recognized by governments in both these countries. Both countries are aware of the potential adverse effect for their levels of foreign direct investment (FDI) and the onus is on Western companies operating in Asia, and other similar environments, to bulk up their risk-management policies and strategies.

Employees in India and China aren't any more dishonest than Westerners, of course, but they are poorer, and they have grown up in a culture lacking any credible deterrent against IP theft. Moreover, if you do not employ staff directly, but rely on subcontractors, then you have few means to incentivize their loyalty to your brand. The cost benefits of offshoring work on sensitive data must be balanced against the premiums required to secure that data. One major issue, for example, will be how far you should integrate your IT systems with those of foreign partners if you don't control the human links in the chain. Some Western software companies split any code they send abroad between multiple engineers. Others use a more expensive type of outsourcing firm (especially popular in India) based on a compound with multiple layers of security and locked-down information systems without ports or drives. In any event, it should be a matter of best practice for transnationals to develop robust internal communications policies and procedures that release valuable data on a need-to-know basis only.

In China, there's an added problem to the protection of ideas – the principle of *guanxi* that has, for centuries, impelled business people to behave properly rather than compelling them, as contract law has done in the West.

To bridge the gap between Western and Eastern views of deal integrity, self-regulating systems of trust are springing up, such as the TrustPass system of the Chinese trading website Alibaba.com. In the coming decades, you should expect to see rating agencies move into this area too, creating profiles of trustworthiness for global supply chains.

Is your worldwide workforce safe from terrorism?

Violent protest is perhaps an unavoidable consequence of democracy, because democracy is based on the rule of the majority. Minorities who cannot further their agenda by political means will always be frustrated, and will always have among them extremists who are willing to resort to violence. Similarly, in the age of globalization, if you are one of a minority who feels their ideas are under threat from global trends such as democracy and free-market capitalism, then you may choose to express that objection through globalized violence, in the manner of Al-Qaeda. What has shocked the world since 9–11 is the increased scale and ruthlessness of terrorist activity: suddenly, everyone is a target, whether you're an Israeli soldier patrolling Gaza or an Italian aid-worker trying to deliver medicine to civilians in the Philippines.

National governments and military regimes have proven incapable of eradicating modern terrorism by conventional means, and there are very few situations in which terrorists can be persuaded to lay down their arms through negotiation. The recent political settlement of The Troubles in Northern Ireland doesn't provide a very useful model for Iraq or Palestine. Why? Because the Irish struggle was predicated on religious sectarianism, not religious fundamentalism. And if God is on your side then why compromise? This anti-humanist doctrine is growing among Christian Evangelicals in the United States as well as the mullahs of the Middle East.

And that's not the only reason why terrorism will remain a problem for individuals and businesses across the world in the coming decades. Western states, and in particular the United States, have now refined the art of conventional warfare to such a degree and built themselves such impressive defensive systems that they are vulnerable only to asymmetric warfare; that is to say, those who feel they can't take on American military forces directly will continue to target civilians and businesses in an effort to exert political pressure or express their religious zeal.

Furthermore, communications advances have made it easier than ever for terrorists to exchange information and materials: in particular, the internet has given everybody in the world the ability to build a bomb from household goods. The infamous *Anarchist Cookbook*, by William Powell, which gave instructions on how to make explosives using simple household items, was first published in 1970. It didn't become infamous until the internet transmitted it into the bedrooms of teenagers all over the world, and two of them – Eric Harris and Dylan Klebold – went on to commit the Columbine High School Massacre. Global communications networks are the very things that have made global terrorism possible, joining disparate cells into perverted 'lifestyle tribes' and, as such, making them impossible for nation states to target directly.

There is very little Western governments can do to counter terrorism in a way that is visible to their own citizens – this is a war that can only be won (or at least, whose adverse effects can only be mitigated) using an asymmetric response, through the infiltration, monitoring and controlled demolition of terrorist networks. So, the visible measures that governments are taking are invariably having an impact on personal freedoms, and on the freedom to do business in certain countries. For example, the US Visitor and Immigrant Status Indicator Technology (US-Visit) programme now requires all non-US citizens entering the United States to have their face photographed and their fingerprints scanned, unless they have a biometric passport issued by a country in the 'US Visa Waiver' programme (ie a friendly country).

As companies increasingly operate internationally, so they must become adept at assessing and tracking the potential terrorist threats they face, building them into risk-management programmes in concert with local authorities, local consulates and embassies – and, if necessary, with third-party security consultants. As well as improving the security of their facilities and procedures for, say, evacuation or alerting emergency services to an attack, they must also be prepared for the possibility of workforce infiltration by terrorists. It's no longer a far-fetched concept, especially if you have facilities that are particularly sensitive, valuable or symbolic of Western affluence. Extra care and attention will have to be paid to the vetting of potential employees, particularly at overseas installations requiring the presence of subcontractors.

Meanwhile, at home, companies of all sizes must prepare for the worst. If national governments and security services are able to improve their protection of soft civilian targets then terrorists will undoubtedly shift their attention to financial or industrial centres, or in the worst-case scenarios to energy sources such as nuclear power stations. In urban areas especially, companies should expect to face periods of major disruption in the coming decades. They must plan for business continuity; mirror their installations if possible to ensure they remain open for business if their headquarters are shut down; arrange for secure remote storage of their business-critical and compliance data; and insure themselves against stoppages.

Evidently, there is still some way to go: research carried out by the cable services provider Cable & Wireless after the London bombings in July 2005 found that 62 per cent of medium-sized businesses in the UK made no provision for staff to work from home in the event of disruption or disaster, while only 29 per cent had updated their business continuity plans since the attacks. It also found that 38 per cent of companies either didn't back up their data or only kept it on-site in the office. Across the West, small and medium-sized companies in particular must be helped by their governments to plan for the protection of their staff and the continuation of trade (or at least, to pick themselves up as quickly as possible).

Political risk: a quick tour of the developing world

How will politics affect business in developing countries in the coming decades? It will depend largely on how successfully they are able to resolve conflicts peacefully, and to defuse the causes of internal unrest. Nevertheless, there are some incipient political trends that enable us to predict what their local business environments will look like in the medium to long term, and what challenges the companies operating there will face.

India

India's development over the next 15 years will be heavily influenced by its relations with Pakistan – the disputed region of Kashmir could even become a flashpoint with China, and while internal ethnic tensions are enough to fuel acts of terrorism, the front-line of the US 'War on Terror' is also close by.

However, the more pressing issue for business in the country is that of infrastructure: or rather, the lack of it. China has levels of road-haulage and air freight many times bigger than those of India, and the proportion of GDP it spends on infrastructure is around three times higher than India's measly 3.5 per cent. Many improvements are under way – for example, the World Bank recently provided India with a £1.7 billion loan to improve six aspects of rural infrastructure, one of which was roads; the state-owned railway system is this year opening its freight services to private competition; and major deals have recently been struck with foreign companies to modernize airports in New Delhi and Mumbai. Morgan Stanley, the global equity company, intends to invest US $7 billion in infrastructure assets in India in 2006/7.

India's political response to wealth inequalities between its regions will have major ramifications for foreign companies operating and investing in the country, in terms of tax regimes, infrastructural development priorities and employment law at both state and federal level. Rather than attempting to compete with China for labour-intensive manufacturing business, the focus will be on developing specialized manufacturing and agribusiness sectors to soak up unskilled workers, while in parallel developing the booming services and hi-tech sectors. There will be the introduction of laws that will liberalize and open up the booming home market so that foreign-owned consumer and retail companies will be able to invest in emerging opportunities.

China

In the coming decades, China's political agenda will be focused on its growing participation in world institutions; preventing North Korea from damaging regional security; and searching continually for new sources of energy. All of these will shape its relations with the United States. It is the last of these issues – energy – that will have the fastest, most direct impact on companies worldwide regardless of other political developments. China's huge thirst for oil could persuade it to engage in economic imperialism, especially in Africa where it is already buying companies and supporting many governments with its aid programmes. The disputed territories with Japan, with their rich gas reserves, could also lead to international tensions. Of equal concern to companies trying to operate in China is the country's banking system which is still undergoing structural reforms to provide a more favourable business environment.

Russia

The economic development of the Russian Federation has in many ways been anarchic. Many entrepreneurs pay off state officials as well as the Mafia, as a matter of course. There are also regional tensions, some based on the desire of certain Russian states for greater autonomy, others based on ethnicity, a threat from Chechnya to the borders of Afghanistan and Iran via Russia's former southern states and the Caspian Sea.

The dilapidated military is no longer equipped to contain all these things, so President Putin has used quasi-totalitarian methods to prevent his administrative processes from spinning out of control. Hopefully this is a short-term measure, but better engagement with Europe will be needed if Russia is truly to embrace the principles of democracy, market economics and the rule of law. What is making this cooperation less likely is the desire of former Soviet states to join Europe against the wishes of their former motherland.

The more likely outcome is that Russia will ally itself with China and countries in Africa in the coming decades, and retain the same style of government. As a result, it will remain sluggish in its development of corporate and commercial law, and leave potential foreign investors wondering how they will be treated if they try to enter its markets. Recent legal aberrations such as the case of former 'oligarch' Mikhail Khordokovsky, and incidents of state coercion such as the bullying of the Ukraine via the apparently deliberate disruption of its Russian gas supply, have all contributed to a feeling that Western companies operating in Russia may be subject to inconsistent and arbitrary treatment. Nevertheless, the Russian government will have little incentive to change in view of its energy resources and continued strong organic growth.

Latin America

The priority for Latin American law-makers over the coming decades will be to sustain growth without the boom-and-bust performance that nearly crippled the region in the 1990s. Many commentators in the region worry that this outlook is endangered by the unrealistic election promises of left-wing governments, which will ultimately lead their voters to insist on a retreat to protectionist policies.

However, the region is enjoying its strongest growth in 25 years, and the International Monetary Fund (IMF) says that it has much greater policy flexibility to protect against external and domestics shocks. The scramble for oil also affects some countries in the region adversely, especially in Central America, while benefiting the oil exporters such as Colombia, Ecuador, Mexico and Venezuela.

Brazil has the highest growth potential thanks to its combination of natural resources, population size and education standards. Also, the present government seems eager to show fiscal discipline, with an emphasis on generating growth by exports rather than the harmful fluctuations of inward investment and consumption it has experienced in the past. However, its business environment is extremely uneven, with over half its 5.3 million companies clustered around the south-western city of São Paolo. Around 45 per cent of Brazil's population lives here, accounting for 60 per cent of the country's GDP. Major investment in infrastructure will therefore be needed to spread both burdens and opportunities nationwide.

The Middle East

The Middle East will obviously continue to have its growth and stability held back by regional tensions – chiefly in the Israel/Palestine region and Iraq. Based on current demographic trends and border positions, Jews will become a minority in Israel by 2020, and this will undoubtedly force a settlement in the region or lead to total catastrophe. However the dispute pans out, the region will continue to be a breeding ground for terrorism, and will therefore continue to face interventions from the United States. A less visible but no less harmful side-effect of the region's turbulence and repression will be the continued 'brain drain' of its best talent to the West, especially female talent.

India and China will have to involve themselves in the region if they wish to satisfy their energy demands by conventional means. As a result of this, and of the region's continued turbulence, the United States and other developed countries will be making massive attempts to diversify their energy portfolios. Indeed, as of 2006, the United States has the stated aim of reducing oil imports from the Middle East by 75 per cent by 2025. Initiatives like this will create pressure for the further development of oil reserves in Russia, Alaska and parts of Africa, as well as stimulating alternative energy research in the West.

Beyond energy, the only things likely to attract FDI to the Middle East will be industries such as construction, project management, hotel management and support services for the expatriate community. Pockets of secular stability will continue to be waypoints for the globe-trotting rich, though here too resentment may be stoked up in the medium to long term by inequality, ultimately challenging a stable business and investment environment.

Africa

Market opportunities for foreign companies will be few and far between, not least because AIDS is decimating Africa's population, even in its more developed areas. However, the region will have an increasing influence over business elsewhere as its energy reserves become more valuable in line with continued turbulence in the Middle East and fossil-fuel scarcity.

At present, many foreign companies that come here do so in order to produce commodities in ways that wouldn't meet the regulatory requirements of more scrupulous nations, for industries such as tobacco and pharmaceuticals. However, an increasing number will be forced to raise their standards in the coming decades by networked consumer boycotting. Agriculture is the one obvious way out for many countries – Kenya, for example, has developed a significant industry in cut flowers. However, for the most part its agribusiness sectors are hamstrung by heavily subsidized Western counterparts; it badly needs Europe to reform its Common Agricultural Policy.

The keys to Africa's development are South Africa, with its comparative stability, high-quality workforce and infrastructure; Uganda, which has recently shown promising signs of growth and technological development under a modernizing elite; and oil-rich Nigeria with its 100-million-strong population. The major obstacle to this development is corruption, which is endemic across the continent.

In the short or medium term, there is little prospect of Africa reducing its overall levels of ethnic tension and military authoritarianism. Accordingly, it will continue to produce millions of unskilled economic migrants. And even in more developed areas, the brain drain of promising young medics, engineers and other skilled workers to the West will continue; in other words, African states will continue to subsidize the workforces of more advanced countries.

The changing role of national governments

As companies become more mobile internationally, so they are becoming more willing – or, indeed, compelled by their shareholders – to move their operations based on the different incentives offered by different national governments. It has therefore become a key responsibility of governments to provide attractive infrastructures, human resources and fiscal environments. In the 20th century, governments were among the biggest providers of economic growth and employment; in the 21st they will chiefly be the facilitators of these things.

The national governments of Continental Europe need to wake up to the fact that some of the luxuries of their social models will be unsustainable in future. The high costs of their worker-friendly policies have already led to job offshoring, and this problem will only be compounded by the growing costs of their ageing populations, not to mention the steps being taken by India and China to boost their home-grown skills. The whole political culture of Europe needs to shift away from 1950s assumptions about jobs for life and generous early-retirement pensions and pump money into support for transferable skills. Research by consulting firm McKinsey recently concluded that transferring from one job to another is much easier in the United States than in Germany because of the way the US labour market is structured and regulated; by contrast, when German companies offshore (mainly to countries in Central and Eastern Europe) the country suffers a much higher proportion of job losses.

This is not to say we should roll back 200 years of improvements to workers' rights and turn Europe back into a low-wage economy. On the contrary, in some areas, heavy state intervention in terms of strict limits on working hours and family-friendly employment legislation is actually generating a competitive advantage – of 91 European regions, two of the most economically vibrant are around Helsinki and Stockholm. It's a matter of creating flexible labour markets and a more enterprising, creative culture that can create products and services that are differentiated in terms of consumer appeal.

Rank	Region
1	Helsinki, Finland
2	Stockholm, Sweden
3	Brussels, Belgium
4	Paris, France
5	Switzerland
6	Luxembourg
7	Hamburg, Germany
8	London, UK
9	Norway
10	Breman, Germany
11	Baden-Werttemberg, Germany
12	South-east, UK
13	Hessen, Germany
14	West-Nederland, Netherlands
15	Bayern, Germany

Source: Robert Huggins Associates 2004

Figure 7.1 Stockholm and Helsinki as the most competitive regions in Europe

Too many national governments are still obsessed with the notion of big industry, largely because big companies generate headline-grabbing blocks of new employment; yet most new employment is of course generated by small companies. Indeed, if you look at the World Economic Forum's index of competitiveness, you'll see that 10 of the top 15 countries are small.

Competitiveness is no longer based on economies of scale. In the coming decades, national governments in the West will have to shift their focus to the creation of highly specialized, highly capable small businesses occupying numerous market niches.

An added benefit here is that entrepreneurs can play a vital role in the cohesion and enhancement of local communities. Large employers are growing more transnational and typically less able to pay attention to the concerns of those living and working

Country	Rank (2004 rank in brackets)
Finland	1 (1)
US	2 (2)
Sweden	3 (3)
Denmark	4 (5)
Taiwan	5 (4)
Singapore	6 (9)
Iceland	7 (6)
Switzerland	8 (7)
Norway	9 (11)
Australia	10 (8)
The Netherlands	11 (12)
Japan	12 (9)
UK	13 (11)
Canada	14 (15)
Germany	15 (13)

Source: World Economic Forum, 2005

Figure 7.2 Competitive nations 2005

immediately around all their facilities; the managers of their individual units tend to have a temporary attitude to the local community. By contrast, the owners of small businesses have always been active in societal terms, not only because they recruit locally but also because they are unlikely to relocate in the short to medium term. In the coming decades, local, regional and state governments will increasingly collaborate with local entrepreneurs in an effort to improve the quality and cohesion of neighbourhoods and communities; and they will be supported in this by national governments, for example in the disbursement of funds for infrastructural development in support of business clusters.

Political pitfalls: the global issues set to distort free trade

In the global knowledge economy, the notion of trade blocs is beginning to look seriously outdated. Arrangements such as the

North American Free Trade Agreement (NAFTA) and the European Common Market are distorting free trade and will continue to do so for as long as their role in macroeconomics is dominated by short-term political interests rather than fairness and equilibrium – necessary conditions if you want a global economy in which 'a rising tide lifts all boats'.

In the coming decades, rich countries will increasingly find it difficult to balance the desire of their citizens to keep traditional industries intact (under the illusion that this will sustain overall levels of employment) while simultaneously importing cheap goods, thereby taking advantage of low-cost, less-protected workforces abroad. Recent trade conflicts such as the one that exploded in late 2005 over the 'Multifibre Agreement', under which the EU imposed textile export quotas on China, will become more frequent – in spite of the fact that such measures divert resources away from the most competitive industries of the protectionist bloc in an effort to prop up the weaker ones, thereby creating a vicious cycle.

With no shared fiscal policy in sight, the dream of a federal Europe is now rapidly giving way to the more realistic prospect of a free-trade zone coupled with a semi-harmonized legal system that allows for diversity while enabling the whole to function (to a diminishing extent) as a trading counterweight to the BRICs (Brazil, Russia, India and China) economies and the United States. The attempt to create a homogenous culture for the EU has failed; if anything, national cultures have strengthened in their resistance to it. Furthermore, the huge disparity in performance between the region's economies, which have tested the original legal parameters of the euro to the limit, will prevent further harmonization and convergence. It was always possible that this disparity would become more pronounced by membership of the single currency, since language differences restrict mobility of labour. For a common market, you really need a common language and culture – the EU apparatus is hugely inefficient primarily because it has to handle such variety. What's more, the UK shows no signs of wishing to join the euro – it is suffering an identity crisis in terms of its relationship with Europe on the one hand and the

United States on the other. Popular culture shapes politics and undoubtedly the popular culture of the UK – celebrities, movies, rock and roll – are US-focused. We watch US-made TV programmes, not French or German. The English language creates a common identity, not an economic union.

In any case, the original goal of the EU, to create a large home market for the manufacturing industries, is no longer necessary; further economic integration would further distort the natural distribution of clusters, resources, talents and capabilities. While the member states of the EU derive some collective bargaining power from the Common Market, they will generate more business in the coming decades by differentiation – that is to say, by investing in specialized industries that have global status.

Ideally, the World Trade Organization (WTO) should render regional trade blocs unnecessary, but so far it has effectively created a trading bloc from the world's richest countries. In the coming decades, it will have to recalibrate its rules to allow the accession of economies that, until recently, were regarded as part of the Third World, if it is to avoid breaking up completely.

Of course, the policing of world trade is directly linked to the policing of world security, and for the next two to three decades there will be only one military force capable of doing such a job. The United States has effectively positioned itself as the world's police force, stoking up envy, resentment and indignation almost everywhere else, and especially in those countries directly affected by the manoeuvres of its armed forces. Some of this bad feeling has stemmed from the tendency of President George W. Bush to link supposed moral imperatives to economic self-interest, and a major knock-on effect has been a resurgence in local pride and consumer boycotting. It's yet another reason why localized brands will fare better than global ones in the coming decades, and why US global brands in particular will be challenged by smaller local rivals.

Nevertheless, many US politicians find the ingratitude of the rest of the world shocking, only 60 years after their parents rescued Europe from Nazism, and then helped to shield it from Soviet aggression and expansion. For them, the United Nations (UN) is nothing but a toothless debating society that expects the

United States to do its dirty work while simultaneously enriching its corrupt members (and even some of its administrators) under the malign indifference of the status quo. At present, the US government feels it is convenient – indeed, expedient – to ignore the UN on certain issues, such as Iraq and Israel. Ironically, the UN will find that the biggest help in the rebuilding of its stature over the coming decades will be the greater balance of power between the United States and China, since there is no equivalent global forum for intergovernmental arbitration.

Can corporate governance really go global?

Many large corporations now seem unaccountable to national governments and their citizens, and to those employees who live in countries where workers have less legal protection. If your corporate turnover is bigger than the GDP of many of the world's economies, then you have the means to circumvent much of the authority of national governments, and may indeed feel compelled to do so in the search for ever-increasing growth on behalf of shareholders.

As supply chains have globalized, so these mega-corporations have come to influence huge numbers of companies and people, and in situations where they prop up local economies the potential for corruption and indifference to workers' rights is high. What's more, it is now common practice to move profits between subsidiaries for tax avoidance purposes; and to deliberately use financial structures that are so complex that auditors and regulators find it difficult to follow the money. The response to these trends in the coming decades will be improved cooperation between Western governments in the short to medium term to strengthen international tax regimes. A crucial part of this will be the harmonization of financial reporting worldwide, through regimes such as the International Financial Reporting Standards (IFRS) adopted widely across the EU in 2005, and the provisions of the US Sarbanes–Oxley (SOX) Act of 2002, also known as the

Public Company Accounting Reform and Investor Protection Act. Many commentators believe that SOX was an overreaction to the scandals at Enron and Worldcom that could actually harm the competitiveness of other US firms. However, the political rationale for the legislation is quite straightforward – the government wanted to make it clear to the world that the United States remained a safe place to invest, in the face of Asian economic growth. Unfortunately, in the coming decades, national regulatory regimes such as these will be incapable of monitoring and controlling the practices and standards of large companies and will need to globalize accordingly.

International groups will soon be the chief monitors of cross-border companies in terms of employment practices, health and safety, environmental impact and even corporate social responsibility (CSR). Initially, they will emerge not from governments but from industry consortia dedicated to self-regulation, who will act chiefly on behalf of well-run Western companies to compel improvements in less-regulated environments such as India, China, Brazil and Russia. Yet in the short term their work will have less of an impact on the most transgressive companies than that of networked independent consumers, who are increasingly taking the regulation of corporate behaviour into their own hands in the face of government impotence and inertia. Here, the internet is proving to be a powerful force.

As educated consumers in the United States and Europe become more affluent and more technologically sophisticated, so they are demanding more information about the provenance of the products they buy, not only to assure themselves of quality but, in the case of a growing minority, to determine the ethical ramifications of that product's manufacture. Did it involve child labour, unregulated pollutants or the economic exploitation of those producing raw materials? Shoppers are becoming less indifferent to questions such as these thanks to improvements in education, information-sharing and a level of affluence that gives them sufficient leisure to care. Consumers in Scandinavia are the leaders in this movement.

The internet has enabled eco-ethical concerns to spread like wildfire. In this way, companies producing everything from foodstuffs and footwear to drugs and electronic products have suffered sales downturns or, in the most serious cases, boycotting of installations. What's more, thanks to a pervasive media – whether in the form of conventional journalism or activist internet posting from the front-line – large companies can't simply sweep such issues under the carpet through the clever use of PR. At least, not as easily as they used to. Witness Nike's continued bad PR for its use of cheap labour in South-east Asia, vociferous protests against Pfizer for its approach to the sale of drugs in Africa, and the failure of Monsanto to recover from its experiments with genetically modified agriculture products in Europe.

Another paradox of globalization is that, while individuals have become more vulnerable to the actions of large corporations, so the latter have become more vulnerable to the actions of individuals. As affluent consumers grow more discriminating in their choice of suppliers on ethical grounds, so national governments will have to respond. Ultimately, when international regulatory agencies are ratified by enough governments, perhaps under the aegis of the UN or the WTO, they will help not only to raise management standards worldwide but also to raise general living standards and equality of opportunity, and even to erode autocratic rule by commercial means. After all, what has had the greater effect on diminishing poverty in India and China? Western charities and government aid programmes or large corporations and their global supply chains? Take a trip to Bangalore or Shanghai and the answer is self-evident.

8 Global remix: the new corporate playlist

The new corporate playlist

- Tackling uncertainty and risk
- Coping with sky-high energy and commodity prices
- Reinventing the global and multinational corporation – towards the globally integrated enterprise
- Managing mergers and acquisitions
- Creating café corporations – the route to creativity, innovation and corporate reinvention
- Leveraging leadership and mucking-out management
- Facing a future of small firms
- Getting to grips with the iPod generation – great talent but not as we know it
- Dealing with the corporate strangers – coping with fear in an age of terror
- Marketing for new markets – out with the old categories

So what does this all mean for us and our businesses? It goes without saying that the 20th-century business models that served us so well will become redundant as the present decade progresses. As the title of this book implies, the reconstitution of the world's economy – as a global remix – will require companies to operate with a new playlist. The old songs, tunes, anthems – call them what you will – will be of little appeal in the 21st century. There is no chance they will make the hit lists. Companies that play the old tunes will perish, as will their employees. They will be like the overwhelming majority of entertainment celebrities – here today but gone tomorrow. Only a few entertainers retain their popularity on a long-term basis. They are only able to do so through constantly reinvesting in their talents and capabilities so that they retain their audience appeal. And so it is and will be with companies, whether they are small businesses or large corporate conglomerates. Corporations, as with celebrities, will need continually to reinvent themselves if they are to survive, let alone prosper, in the fundamentally changing social, economic, demographic and political environment of the 21st century. To summarize the issues in this book, there are 10 tracks that will make up the corporate playlist of the 21st century.

Tackling uncertainty and risk

Doing business in the 21st century is going to be tough. The internet revolution has created an interconnected global economy. This has opened up unprecedented markets but it has also created greater risks and uncertainties for doing business. In the past, companies expanded in markets with well-established legal frameworks and legitimated political orders. Today, business opportunities are in the BRICs (Brazil, Russia, India and China) economies, each of which has weaknesses in its compliance and regulatory regimes. What this means for businesses is that they will have to reassess their risk management strategies. They will need to be less risk averse and, like their smaller business partners, be more adventurous and entrepreneurial. Rather like the Vikings and Christopher Columbus, they will have to sail into the unknown if they are to gain the riches and defeat their competitors. Matters will only be made worse (or better) by growing geopolitical uncertainties. There are social tensions of a varying kind in many of the emerging markets that will add to the complexities of doing business in the 21st century. Continuing uncertainties in the Middle East, the War on Terror and the emergence of fundamentalism create scenarios that could generate serious economic discontinuities.

What this means is that corporate scenario planning will be more complex and many companies will be inclined to develop more cautious, short-term investment strategies. These will be the companies that will not survive. The rewards will go to the more adventurous, self-confident CEOs who recognize the need for reinvented business decision-making and more entrepreneurial corporate cultures to realize the opportunities available in the uncertain world of the 21st century.

Coping with sky-high energy and commodity prices

The industrialization of the West was on the back of cheap energy and commodity prices. Both directly and indirectly, the economies of Europe and the United States have benefited from past colonialism, with continents carved up and countries created according to the West's commodity and energy needs. Iraq, large parts of the Middle East and Africa are examples of this. In the 21st century, economic growth on the basis of cheap energy and commodity prices is coming to an end. Over the next 50 years or so – unless new resources are discovered – the world is likely to run out of both oil and gas. The demands of China for energy and commodity resources to fuel its continuing dynamic economic growth are bound to inflate energy prices in unprecedented ways. How can it be otherwise when a country of 1.3 billion people aspires to have First World living standards? Some estimates suggest that China will consume one-third of the world's energy resources by 2030. And this, in turn, is already beginning to have repercussions for the world's political order. China is buying up Angola's oil and negotiating similar deals in Venezuela. Will its search for this resource bring it into conflict with Japan (over offshore resources in the sea between the two countries) and with the United States?

But it is not only oil and China. There is also Russia and its natural resources and the raw materials of Africa and South America that the BRICs economies will consume to fuel their economic growth. With high economic growth rates in these countries, there can be little alternative to big increases in energy and commodity prices over the next decades. If India and China have, up until now, had deflationary impacts upon Western economies through their provision of cheap manufacturing products, their impact during the 21st century will be inflationary. Their continuing growth will force up energy and commodity prices around the world.

What this means for the corporate playlist is higher energy bills and increased production costs. Consumer demand in the mature domestic markets is likely to be dampened by virtue of a higher percentage of household and personal incomes being devoted to energy and fuel bills. The search for alternative, sustainable fuel resources becomes a top priority for both governments and global energy companies as we proceed into the 21st century.

Reinventing the global and multinational corporation – towards the globally integrated enterprise

The historical growth of companies has been to saturate domestic markets and then to move overseas, or alternatively, to develop international patterns of trading through importing raw materials, products and semi-finished components for final assembly, distribution and sale. Either way, there has been the growth of global supply chains, arranged and integrated by corporate HQs that retain their nerve centres in their homelands. The essential 'national character' of these multinational or global corporations is reflected in the composition of their boards of directors and senior executive teams. IBM and Microsoft have remained essentially American while Siemens is German; Philips, Dutch; Nokia, Finnish; and so on. These corporate nerve centres retain control over strategic decision-making, R&D, business planning, merger and acquisition (M&A) strategies, etc. What is distributed to other countries – particularly emerging markets – is low-skill, low-wage production activities.

In the 21st century, this is potentially a recipe for disaster with wide-ranging political consequences. The structuring of companies in this way leads to an awareness of cross-national exploitation and inequality both among employees and in their wider societies. It fuels the development of extreme political movements and the election of radical national governments that cultivate votes on the basis of anti-capitalist/US/West political tickets. The outcomes can range from selling oil to China instead of to Western companies through to nationalization and the imposition of high taxes and regulatory controls.

This is why wise multinational companies of the 21st century will evolve into globally integrated enterprises (GIEs). IBM, early in 2006, announced that it is to invest US $10 billion in developing R&D, designs and other 'brain' activities in India over the next few years. It intends to break up its US-based knowledge operations and distribute these to other countries. Through the capabilities of information and communication technologies, these can be coordinated to develop and deliver products and services for both global and local markets. Through this approach, new career routes are opened up within the company that are truly international/global, offering opportunities for employees located in various countries who are presently 'excluded' from these 'core' corporate functions. More companies will evolve their operating processes in this way, creating cultural diversity and making themselves genuinely international businesses. In this way, large global and multinational corporations will be more sustainable. In any case, it is likely that the burgeoning economies of India, China and Asia will compel them to shift their centres of corporate activity to these regions of the world.

What this means is that corporate executives of the future, together with their key operating colleagues – the 'celebrities' and the loyal 'lieutenants' – will be more mobile as either expatriates or inpatriates as well as being recruited from more diverse backgrounds. It will be a challenge for HR directors to develop strong corporate cultures that genuinely incorporate and harmonize cultural practices rather than simply imposing US and European models of management upon their wealth-generating subsidiary companies.

Managing mergers and acquisitions

An interconnected world has opened up more opportunities for corporate M&As. The continuing sophistication of information and communication technologies allows business processes to be integrated on a global basis and for supply chains, consisting of separate but coordinated operating units, to be managed as effectively as on a single site. If your business has developed such expertise, why not continue to grow through even more acquisitions? But there are also other factors encouraging global M&As, namely the increasing harmonization of business practices and the adoption of global technology and quality standards. The culture of a 'global media village' facilitates the integration of corporate cultures brought about by M&A activity.

The continuing intensity of M&A activity creates greater uncertainties. The threat of being taken over puts added pressures on CEOs – the corporate celebrities – to hit or surpass performance targets. It leads to a focus on short-term gains – Q1, Q2, Q3, etc – to keep shareholders happy, such as financial institutions and private equity funds. The loyal lieutenants are only too aware of the possible outcome of being targeted as a takeover bid – job loss. It has happened to their friends, parents and former colleagues. The result is that M&As create not only cultures of uncertainty but also cynical attitudes towards their employers. They may pay lip service to commitment, loyalty and dedication but, beneath this veneer, there lurks a darker psychology. It takes a strong corporate culture and a highly incentivized reward system to compensate for these activities and to preserve the degree of commitment necessary for high performance.

What this means is that M&As, driven for all kinds of reasons – many of which are often later proven to be unproductive – are forcing employees at all levels to be risk averse. They do not want to be among the first to be shown the door come the post-merger rationalization. In a lifetime of expensive home loans and family commitments, compliance with corporate values is the better way to behave. It is not advisable to be innovative, creative and to put forward 'out of the box' suggestions for changing things. To do so can be interpreted as being challenging, critical and, even, 'undermining'. Essentially, the risk of being taken over encourages colleagues to 'keep their heads down'.

Creating café corporations – the route to creativity, innovation and corporate reinvention

Future organizations will have to abandon their traditional management structures, that is, their operational processes based on hierarchical control and the specialist division of operational job tasks. These structures were and are entirely appropriate for the large-scale production of standardized products and services. What is demanded of employees in these businesses is that they carry out their tasks in an entirely pre-dictable and routine fashion, producing consistency of output, in terms of both quality and quantity. The creative employee is a nuisance; to suggest new and different ways of doing things is often counterproductive to operating efficiencies. What managers hope for most of all is that their reportees will turn up for work and 'just get on with it'. Cost is the optimum consideration and, in the 21st century, costs are much lower in the BRICs economies and other emerging markets. That's why, of course, there is the shift of the manufacturing of commoditized products to these countries.

What's left for Western companies is the need to develop specialized, high-value products and services for the mature economies as well as for expanding groups of affluent consumers in the emerging markets of the world. The future is with professional service organizations – whether it is Coca-Cola, Pfizer, Motorola or a media corporation such as the BBC. The operating core for these organizations, and the basis for their high performance and competitive advantage, is leveraging creativity. This is why traditional management models are inappropriate. Highly skilled scientists, R&D personnel, professionals and those with technical and imaginative expertise cannot be *told* to be creative and innovative. Innovation and creativity cannot be designed as routine productive processes in the same way that cars can be manufactured.

Ideas, imagination, creativity and the innovative products that follow can only be facilitated, not managed. This means the modern corporation has to take on the qualities of the medieval village square or the present-day café. Architecture, facilities, design and location have to be organized in such ways that colleagues have the capacity to argue, discuss, experiment and challenge. Out of these discourses, the rollout of innovative products and services flows, from TV programmes and management consultancy advice to marketing re-launches and innovative sales campaigns.

What this means is that knowledge-based businesses have to encourage flexible, remote and other working practices that are appropriate to colleagues, according to their individual preferences and needs. But, alongside this provision, corporations have to redesign their workplaces as cafés to encourage the exchange of ideas and informal collaboration in the development of projects, products and services. It is back to the coffee shops of Dr Johnson in the 18th century. Or, even, the medieval village square where the carpenter, blacksmith and farmer met to discuss the design and manufacture of a farm gate. This requires a shift of business leadership style; one that is self-confident and relaxed, but sets tight parameters in relation to performance targets and time and cost budgets.

Leveraging leadership and mucking-out management

There is hardly a business school that doesn't offer MBA modules and executive programmes in leadership. Many of these have merely substituted 'leadership' for 'management'. Otherwise, the course content taught by the same faculty teachers seems about the same. As long as the fees roll in to bankroll other parts of the university – the Philosophy and Theology departments – who cares? But they should care.

As discussed in this book, leadership and management reflect two quite distinct and separate approaches to organizations. In the 21st century, growing geopolitical and economic uncertainties are compelling CEOs – as corporate celebrities – to create scenarios of future trends and then, on the basis of these, to offer a vision for the future of their businesses. From this, strategies follow which are implemented as operational plans and targets.

The common assumption that stems from this way of thinking is that leadership should be located at the top of the company and that, below this, management is the preferred methodology for getting tasks accomplished. Far from it. The high-performing 21st-century organization demands leadership at every level. As discussed earlier, ideas and imagination have to be carefully nurtured and facilitated in directions that lead to product innovation. Instead of destroying individuality, it should be stretched to the limit – and for the good of the company.

What this means for organizations is that corporate management training programmes need to be reassessed. But, more than this, leaders need to ask themselves why should their employees want to admire, trust and be inspired by them? Often difficult questions to answer, but only positive responses offer the key to effective leadership and high innovative performance. Ask the entrepreneur leader of any small firm.

Facing a future of small firms

Bill Gates says that the future lies with small firms. On balance, he is probably right. He was not referring to the large-scale mass commodity producers of India, China and other emerging markets. He was implicitly, if not explicitly, discussing the future of the knowledge-based economies of the West.

It is in small firms that leadership is most likely to flourish, rather than bureaucratic rule-bound management. Admiration, imagination and trust can be more easily developed within the context of small economic units, based, as they are, on face-to-face relations among a small number of colleagues. These businesses are likely to be fit (lean cost structures to be competitive), fresh (constant experimentation and innovative) and fun (the driver of fitness and freshness). Unless colleagues enjoy their jobs, they are hardly likely to be innovative and cost-conscious. This simple point is something that *management* consultants often fail to understand as they attempt to impose structures and procedures upon what appears to them to be chaotic or, at best, *ad hoc* activities that often characterize the fast-growing small firm. Instead of building and leveraging upon what is already there, they impose 'big business templates' and, through these, destroy the 'fun' and, therefore, the 'fit' and 'fresh' attributes of these businesses.

Small-firm leadership captures employee inspiration, commitment and, with luck, excitement. It is through these attributes that small businesses have rich textures of social and emotional relationships which, in creating tacit knowledge, explain their high performance.

But can these attributes be adopted by large companies? According to Jack Welch, ex-CEO of GE, they can. In his view, these corporations need to be broken down into small business operating units. Trading under global brands, these constellations or conglomerations of small business units are the survival route of the future. It is only by corporate restructuring and creating small business units that large companies will have the capacity to reinvent themselves. This is through inspirational leadership, emotionally committed colleagues and the subsequent rollout of a steady stream of innovative products and services.

What this means is that large companies in the knowledge-based economies of the West need to restructure, re-culture and take on all the attributes of small firms. As stated in a previous track, experts, creatives, scientists, technologists, etc, will not be told what to do. Well, they can be, but they then simply carry out their tasks and keep their own innovative and creative ideas to themselves. The entrepreneurial leader – as distinct from the corporate manager – is less likely to get this reaction. Why? Because, as a leader, the business is organized on the basis of admiration, inspiration and trust. Ask Richard Branson about his early days.

Getting to grips with the iPod generation – great talent but not as we know it

A demographic timebomb is hitting the economies of the West. We are aware of the ageing population but, alongside this, there is a shortage of young people coming into labour markets. In the United States, these will increasingly be Spanish-speaking Hispanics, while in Europe there are real problems on the horizon. So far, these have been avoided through the inward migration of young people from the accession states to the 'Old Europe' countries of the European Union. Women are having fewer children and at a later age.

More young people attend universities and institutions of higher education than ever before. If ever there were a link between talent and qualification, this has been made tenuous by governments' commitment to expand higher education opportunities. No longer can companies assume that university graduates have employable skills. High-performing companies demand additional qualities. They want potential employees with imagination and ideas that will make up the talent pools for future innovation and growth. Do universities encourage these qualities? Some do, but on the whole it is left to a minority of elite institutions to perform this task. But there is also the bedroom.

Many parents have teenage and younger children who spend quite a lot of their time in their bedrooms. They respond to parental commands through text messaging, e-mails and, occasionally, grunts. Parents with children of this kind should be congratulated for bringing up normal, well-adjusted youngsters. But they fear for their children's futures. Will they ever be employable? But – what is going on in the bedroom?

More often than not, the unleashing of talents far greater than those of their parents when they were of a similar age. Some of them are producing their own music CDs; not simply downloading them but actually *creating* them. Others are doing the same with DVDs, while even others are playing games on the internet, assembled in global-based virtual teams. This is a present fashion in the Scandinavian countries.

How do companies capture and retain these creative talents? Certainly not by operating according to the management paradigms of today's companies. The jobs offered are seen by young people as boring, with limited capabilities for personal development, excitement and capability.

What this means is that companies will have to change. As discussed earlier, they will need to be café corporations. But, more than that, they will have to tolerate non-conformity and individuality in terms of attitudes, behaviour, dress codes and lifestyles. Small businesses are more likely to allow for these personal differences than large companies. That's why the iPod generation is more attracted to working in small firms; they are given more space and personal autonomy. It is another reason why the corporate elephants need to imitate the entrepreneurial fleas.

Understanding the corporate strangers – coping with fear in an age of terror

Globalization consists of supply chains that cut across national boundaries and interconnect First and Third World countries.

But it is more than this; the mobility of commodities and services is also reinforced by the mobility of labour. According to some UN estimates, there are more than 200 million economic migrants in the world today. These are men, women (and, appallingly, children) who are forced to leave their home countries and work in other places to escape, quite literally, starvation. It is bad enough being poverty stricken but it is even worse when modern communications let you know that there are other parts of the world where wealth is in abundance.

The globalization of labour markets has created diversity within the major cities of the world. Twenty-seven per cent of London's residents, for instance, were born outside the UK. The composition of corporate payrolls also echoes similar patterns of diversity. Again, in London, no fewer than 76 per cent of those working in the hospitality industry do not have English as their first language.

With these trends, it is imperative that modern corporations embrace cultural diversity; that they are inclusive, providing equal opportunities for all ethnic, national, religious and gender groups. More than this, cultural diversity creates more imaginative mind-sets and corporate cultures that are less introspective. It is only necessary to point to the entertainment, fashion and sport industries to understand how embracing cultural diversity encourages genuine global cultures that lead to world-class performance.

But there is another aspect of globalization that poses dangers to the modern corporation. This is the movement of talented, technical and creative experts from one business to the next. For many, corporate loyalty counts for nothing; they perceive their tenure as short-term for the purposes of gaining as much personal reward in as brief a time as possible. This can have outcomes for the protection of corporate databases, intellectual property rights and other knowledge resources that make up a company's competitive advantage. In a world of corporate travellers, we are often not aware of the background and, more importantly, the allegiances of colleagues who may occupy key positions in corporate structures.

What this means is that companies in the globalized economy of the 21st century must create cultures and opportunity structures that are inclusive and which embrace diversity. This is why there is no option for multinational businesses but to evolve into globally integrated enterprises. It can no longer be assumed that employee allegiance can be purchased through the payroll. Priority has to be given to cementing the psychological contract so that there is genuine employee commitment. The protection of corporate intellectual property rights requires more than security checks at the office gates.

Marketing for new markets – out with the old categories

Major drivers for corporate reinvention are the greater competitive threats through the globalization of markets. Small businesses located on the other side of the world can market and sell their products and services in the West as though customers were at their geographical back door. In the south-east of England, there is a shed – it is no more than that – which sells 1920s English household artefacts: bath tubs, radiators, cookers, etc. It looks as though it relies on front-door, face-to-face, passing trade for its customers. The reality is that 80 per cent of its goods for sale are made in China and 70 per cent of these are sold to online customers in the United States. In other words, the business is essentially – contrary to all appearances – an internet trader.

Emerging markets are also creating new categories of mass consumers. Today in India there are 70 million men and women with an average income of US $25,000 per annum. Estimates for China suggest a similar figure. This is why these two countries can no longer be regarded as locations for cheap production but as growing markets of consumer spend. This is why Western retail, media and fashion companies are now rushing to set up trading outlets in these countries. It is the tastes of consumers in these emerging markets that will shape the design and functionality of many products in the future and, hence, the R&D and innovation strategies of

Western-based companies. This is already happening at Unilever and Proctor & Gamble.

In the mature consumer markets of the West, the old marketing categories no longer apply. The age, occupation and income of consumers are of declining relevance in shaping their spending patterns. We are in an era of liberated consumers who, through affiliation to lifestyle tribes, express identities through brand purchases. The exciting dimension of this trend is that lifestyle affiliation is essentially transient as consumers constantly experiment and change.

What this means is that consumer-focused businesses, with the knock-on effects for their partners in supply chains, have continually to anticipate future trends. The danger is to be too *close* to the customer, meeting the demands of today but failing to anticipate what these are likely to be in the future. This was the problem of UK-based Marks & Spencer in the 1990s. Its detailed knowledge of customers did not enable it to understand how these would change as a result of changing lifestyles. Consumers do not know what they will want in the future. Ten years ago, we did not know that we would want to book airline tickets and holidays online. We did not know that we wanted to auction our personal effects to people living on the other side of the world. High-performing companies anticipate and create demands. The challenge for businesses of all shapes and forms is to anticipate socio-economic, demographic and technological trends.

These are the key issues that make up the new corporate playlist. The remix of the global economy has ramifications for all aspects of business. In a century of increasing risk and uncertainty, the knock-on effects for our futures and working lives are difficult to comprehend fully. For some, the future will seem daunting or even frightening. But, for others prepared to embrace the opportunities offered by the brave new world of the 21st century, there cannot be a better time to be in business. Even our favourite CD tracks can become boring. Today, we can constantly remix and reconstruct our music playlists. So it is with business in the 21st century. Welcome to this exciting new world!

Index